"Abraham Kuyper was a profound theologian, an encyclopedic thinker, and a deeply spiritual man who believed that it is the believer's task 'to know God in *all* his works.' In a day when secular science is seeking to establish hegemony over all knowing, and when postmodern art is threatening to bring an end to art, Kuyper's solid, Biblical insights can help to restore perspective and sanity to these two critical areas of human life."

Chuck Colson
Founder, Prison Fellowship and the
Colson Center for Christian Worldview

"The appearance of this treatise in English translation is for me the beginning of a larger dream come true. Kuyper's writings on common grace are much needed 'for such a time as this' and *Wisdom & Wonder* is a marvelous foretaste of more that is to come!"

Richard J. Mouw
president and professor of Christian philosophy,
Fuller Theological Seminary

"Abraham Kuyper's *Wisdom & Wonder* is an eloquent theological antidote to the anti-intellectualist and anti-artistic impulses that infect so much of the contemporary church. Kuyper issues a clarion call for Christians to move beyond Bible study and theology, and beyond church art, to engage in these graced endeavors (science and art) in gratitude to God and out of fidelity to Christian conviction. Though Kuyper wrote these words more than one hundred years ago, they have lost none of their bite and relevance."

Nicholas Wolterstorff
Noah Porter Professor Emeritus of Philosophical Theology,
Yale University
Senior Fellow, Institute for Advanced Studies in Culture,
University of Virginia

"How do we make sense of the contributions of, say a Steve Jobs, to human culture? How do Christians account for the rather immeasurable amount of good achieved by those presumably uncovenanted with God? Common grace is the answer: God's mercies are over all his works. This first-ever English translation of Abraham Kuyper's work on common grace hits the sweet spot for Christians seeking answers to questions about the breadth of the gospel, their own roles in public life, and the beneficial contributions of others, especially in science and art. Highly needed and recommended."

David K. Naugle
distinguished university professor, Dallas Baptist University
author of *Worldview: The History of a Concept*

"'What do you possess that you did not first receive?' asks St. Paul (1 Cor. 4:7). In other words, *everything* is grace—in one sense. But if that is so, what happens to the distinctive grace of the gospel? It is the great merit of the neo-Calvinist Abraham Kuyper that he addressed that knotty problem in ways that still command attention. This new translation of *Wisdom & Wonder* will help all Christians keep their confessional distinctiveness while remaining open to the world. Here is salt that has not lost its tang."

Edward T. Oakes, SJ
professor of systematic theology, University of St. Mary of the Lake

"The essays translated in this volume represent Kuyper's mature and comprehensive thought on science and the arts in general—a coherent position grounded in Calvinist theology and demonstrating a keen understanding of the cultural currents of his day. They set a provocative example that Christian thinkers should try to match in our own day."

James Bratt, professor of history, Calvin College
editor of *Abraham Kuyper: A Centennial Reader*

"Abraham Kuyper thought big even when he considered little things. He challenges us to recognize the Creator as Lord, not simply of some 'spiritual' part of his world, but of it all. Here, in this beautifully presented volume, we are invited to listen afresh to Kuyper's wisdom and vision; his words are worth wrestling through today just as they were when he first wrote them."

Kelly M. Kapic
professor of theological studies, Covenant College

"C. S. Lewis suggested that for every new book, we should read three old ones. Kuyper is one of those authors we should read. Although he's familiar to many who have explored worldview thinking, few have actually read him and until now even fewer have had the opportunity to read this particular work. Given the consistent battles of definitions that take place in art and the sciences, we need trusted voices from the past to guide us. I'm grateful that the Acton Institute and Kuyper College have made this available."

John Stonestreet
Summit Ministries, Colson Center for Christian Worldview

"Young Christians, take heart: we stand in a long tradition of those who seek a fully-orbed faith. Kuyper's clear, friendly, theologically deep approach is a century-old answer to questions we're still grappling with—how we ought to live in and work with the natural world and the culture we humans build. This volume is invaluable to anyone who wants to glean from and build upon Kuyper's important, foundational work."

Alissa Wilkinson
coeditor, *Comment*
founding editor, *Curator* magazine

C

WISDOM & WONDER

WISDOM & WONDER

COMMON GRACE in SCIENCE & ART

ABRAHAM KUYPER

EDITED BY JORDAN J. BALLOR AND STEPHEN J. GRABILL
TRANSLATED BY NELSON D. KLOOSTERMAN

WITH AN INTRODUCTION BY VINCENT E. BACOTE
AND A FOREWORD BY GABE LYONS AND JON TYSON

Christian's LIBRARY PRESS

GRAND RAPIDS · MICHIGAN

For information please email customerservice@russell-media.com.

Library of Congress Control Number: 2011938299

ISBN (paperback): 978-1-937498-90-0
ISBN (hardback): 978-1-937498-96-2

Christian's Library Press
An imprint of the Acton Institute for the Study of Religion & Liberty
161 Ottawa Ave. NW, Suite 301
Grand Rapids, Michigan 49503
Phone: 616.454.3080
Fax: 616.454.9454
www.clpress.com

Manuscript preparation, design, and layout provided by
http://www.russell-media.com

Cover design by Brandon Hill
Interior design by Sharon Page
Editorial assistance provided by Dylan Pahman

Printed in the United States of America

For Dr. Rimmer de Vries,

In recognition of your lifetime pursuits and enduring legacy as a cultural leader, economist, visionary, and faithful follower of Christ, who reflects well the Kuyperian vision of Christ's lordship over all spheres of society

CONTENTS

FOREWORD

Followers of Jesus face numerous challenges in our current time, not the least of which is themselves.

Life in western culture is being increasingly described as "secular," "amoral," and "godless," even as many of God's faithful scramble to make sense of a public square that seems to have gone terribly awry. It is not as if a certain aspect of our faith is being challenged, but the plausibility of faith itself has no credibility as we come to terms with life in a pluralistic society. Whatever faith we have left often feels like a hangover from another time, instead of a robust faith that informs the whole of our lives today. But is the problem with followers of Jesus *themselves*?

We are reminded of Walt Kelly's famous words, "I have met the enemy, and he is us!" Christians today face a serious framework challenge from within. We have lost a coherent, holistic understanding of how the Gospel, and thereby the practice of the Christian faith, relates to every single area of society. Our confidence has been shaken to the roots as we struggle to offer an alternative reality to a longing world.

Enter Abraham Kuyper.

Like many, we were first introduced to Kuyper's work indirectly through famed evangelical Chuck Colson when he exclaimed in his book, *How Now Shall We Live?*, that "Christians are called to redeem entire cultures, not just individuals."

That single declaration changes everything. It reveals a truth that many Christians have forgotten, that we as Christians have a role, indeed a responsibility, to be involved in renewing every realm of the world. Nothing is to be left untouched by the transformative power of the Gospel. This was the influence of Kuyper.

Kuyper reminds us—in a time when many Christians unknowingly live dualistic, disintegrated lives—that the whole of life, not just the "spiritual parts," belong to God. Dallas Willard, among others, properly diagnoses the problem when he describes the "truncated gospel" adopted by many. In this flawed, reductionist view, rather than living out of the riches of the full biblical narrative of Creation, Fall, Redemption, and Restoration, Christians grapple with only the themes of Fall (sin) and Redemption (the cross). This often leaves us confused, questioning whether it is possible to see beauty and goodness in a world pervasively marred by sin. It causes us to miss out on much of the work God is up to in the world. When we do this, we reduce the scale of the work of God to withdrawing, waiting, and evacuating. We are left struggling to be fully present in the world, believing that God will ultimately abandon it in favor of a spiritual realm.

Kuyper, on the other hand, believes and teaches that the whole of creation until its full consummation belongs to God. He is not just the Lord of heaven, but also the Lord of heaven *and* earth. As the Psalmist puts it, *the earth is the Lord's and the fullness thereof.* God's work of creation continues even today in the fullness and joy of all human life and culture. It is this coherent understanding and practical sensibility about faith's application in all of life that leaves Kuyper's readers with the ultimate epiphany.

Why Science and Art?

In *Wisdom & Wonder*, Kuyper addresses two of the more difficult realms that intimidate Christians in modern-day conversations: science and art.

Many Christians feel threatened by science, and believe it is not trustworthy and poses an affront to faith. Issues surrounding bioethics, evolution, environmental stewardship, and the probability of more scientific discovery through new technologies all cloud our objectivity about right and wrong, good and evil.

Art is another aspect in which Christians have an uneasy, ill-defined relationship. We live in a time when our imaginations are under assault, and creativity has become a casualty in many of our lives. We are not trained to recognize good art from poor and our patronage of good culture is being all but lost. Sadly, much of the art Christians do appreciate is classified as "Christian art," yet does little to move us deeply. Kuyper comes alongside helping us retrieve the notion that great art should not only touch our hearts but also engage our minds. If it fails to do so it is not artful.

Kuyper's insistence that Jesus really is Lord of all bounces off the pages of this book. His conviction that science is not a threat to our faith, but an ally, and his exhortations to celebrate the glory of God through creative expression will joyfully cause many to add new words of praise to the Lord of both heaven and earth.

Gabe Lyons
Founder, Q Ideas & author, *The Next Christians*
Jon Tyson
Pastor, Trinity Grace Church & author, *Rumors of God*

TRANSLATOR'S PREFACE

Translating a book across time and across languages is never a perfectly smooth process. Therefore, we need to clarify for our readers a number of translation and editorial decisions that should enhance this translation of a Dutch work authored more than one hundred years ago. These decisions, naturally, involve alterations, subtractions, and additions.

For example, when citing Scripture, Kuyper employed either the Dutch *Staten Vertaling* or his own paraphrase of the text. Consistent with our goal of producing a contemporary English translation of this work, we have used the English Standard Version (ESV) of the Bible, unless otherwise noted. To aid the reader, at some points we have replaced Kuyper's paraphrase with the actual text of the ESV, and we have also supplied (in parentheses) the specific textual references, which were absent from the original, of either Scripture citations or paraphrases. For some references and allusions that may be unfamiliar, we have added limited notes with references to the related texts of Scripture.

Brief editorial notes have been added throughout, in order to identify persons, schools of thought, or events mentioned in the original that might be unfamiliar to contemporary readers.

Other stylistic alterations have been made, for ease of reading and for the sake of appearance. Italics are used less frequently in the translation than appear in the original. More importantly, large paragraphs and long sentences have been divided, and subordinate clauses have occasionally been rearranged to render accurately the emphasis present in Kuyper's original. Chapter titles, as well as part divisions, have also been added. The original title of the volume in Dutch appears here as the subtitle, and we have added a new title, *Wisdom & Wonder*, to try to capture the essence of Kuyper's message.

Bringing significant intellectual works into the modern day by way of translation frequently confronts the translator and editor with matters involving sensitive sociocultural views and associated language. As times change, so do modes of expression. This pertains to Kuyper's work as well. For example, where possible we have opted for a responsible, though by no means rigorous, use of gender-neutral nouns and pronouns (for example, speaking of "people" rather than "men"). Where necessary and only infrequently, infelicitous formulations have either been altered for the modern ear or omitted altogether.

Perhaps the most significant translation challenge involves rendering the Dutch word *wetenschap* in ways suited to Kuyper's use and context. The basic meaning of the word is simply *knowledge*, but in contexts of academic and philosophical usage, it corresponds to the German word *Wissenschaft*, referring to *science*.

In contrast to modern notions of science, however, Kuyper understood science in a broad sense to refer to something belonging to creation, something God made, to which the Creator assigned a unique calling. Kuyper was fully aware that science consisted of human reflection upon creation, but insisted that such human reflection mirrored or imitated the divine thought embedded in all creation. In Kuyper's view, science is an ever-growing body of knowledge and insight that was called into being by God, undergoes development throughout history by people devoted to its study, and can be restored and sanctified in Jesus Christ. The modern view of science, however, usually employs the term *science* with reference to a neutral rational method of inquiry, and with reference to specific disciplines or domains.

Moreover, Kuyper distinguished between "lower science" and "higher science"; the former refers to simple, direct human observation of phenomena in creation, while the latter refers to more refined reflection on and practice of scientific inquiry in terms of a system. In addition to the natural sciences (what we might term the hard sciences or the exact sciences), Kuyper spoke of the spiritual sciences, or what today are distinguished as the humanities and the social sciences (literature, poetry, history, psychology, anthropology, sociology, economics, and so on.). Keeping these differences in mind should assist the reader in properly understanding Kuyper's wide-ranging use of the term.

Finally, we would mention our grateful use at several points of the partial translation of the section dealing with common grace and science included in *Abraham Kuyper: A Centennial Reader*, edited by James D. Bratt (Grand Rapids: Wm. B. Eerdmans, 1998, pp. 442-460), which was based on a reworking of material produced by Hans van de Hel. A special word of thanks is due to Clifford Anderson, George Harinck, and Harry Van Dyke for their expert advice and assistance at various points in the preparation of this text.

Nelson D. Kloosterman
16 August 2011

INTRODUCTION
Vincent E. Bacote

Abraham Kuyper (1837-1920) was a remarkable Dutch figure whose life and work remains relevant today, particularly because of the ongoing ferment regarding the proper role of Christians in public life. Kuyper was the son of a minister and pursued higher education at the University of Leiden. Strongly influenced by modern thought, he eventually entered pastoral ministry in the rural town of Beesd, where he underwent a conversion to orthodox Christianity through the influence of some pietistic and confessionally Reformed members of his congregation. During this same period, Kuyper's interest in a faith with public impact began to emerge.

While he was deeply appreciative for all he learned from his parishioners, he was also aware that Christianity was not only reserved for the internal chambers of the heart but also determinative for the various social dimensions of life humans encounter as they participate in the realms of culture, politics, and economics. Eventually Kuyper became a leader in the Anti-Revolutionary (as in French Revolution) movement (it became a political party by 1879), and became the editor of daily (*De Standaard*) and weekly (*De Heraut*) newspapers.

Kuyper directed his attention toward issues related to the internal politics of the national church of the Netherlands (*Nederlandse Hervormde Kerk* or NHK) and eventually became involved in national politics in 1874. He saw himself as an advocate for orthodox Christians who were marginalized from public influence and sought to make a case for Christian influence in the public square, as exemplified by his support of expanding the vote to all households and the public support of Christian schools. He helped to found the Free University of Amsterdam in 1880, where he also taught theology.

After a great ecclesiastical crisis, he led the 1886 separation from the NHK (the *Doleantie*, or "grieving ones"); in 1892 this group united with those churches who had already seceded from the NHK in 1834 (the *Afscheiding*, or "separated ones"). The 1890s saw Kuyper increasing in influence; he gave the Stone Lectures at Princeton Theological Seminary in 1898 and, in part due to a coalition with Catholic members of Parliament, he became Prime Minister of the Netherlands from 1901 to 1905. Wearing the hats of pastor, theologian, journalist, and politician at various times in his life, Kuyper embodied a commitment to public Christianity while maintaining a fervent personal piety (as revealed by his devotional writing).

> SPHERE SOVEREIGNTY IS KUYPER'S IDEA THAT FROM GOD'S SOVEREIGNTY THERE DERIVES MORE DISCRETE SOVEREIGN "SPHERES" SUCH AS THE STATE, BUSINESS, THE FAMILY, AND THE CHURCH.

While Kuyper is known for his approach to a number of theological issues, perhaps the most prominent are sphere sovereignty, antithesis, and common grace. Sphere sovereignty is Kuyper's idea that from God's sovereignty there derives more discrete sovereign "spheres" such as the state, business, the family, and the church. He also used this idea to help make the case for distinctive Christian public institutions such as schools and hospitals. Sphere sovereignty describes a pluralism of both social structures and worldviews and is one prominent feature in Kuyper's approach to public life.

The emphasis on Christian distinctiveness is also rooted in Kuyper's view of the antithesis between Christians and those not regenerated by the Holy Spirit. As *Wisdom & Wonder* reveals at certain points, Kuyper believed that regeneration yields a distinct epistemological difference that ultimately leads Christians to interpret reality differently (and with better precision) than non-Christians. When emphasizing the antithesis, Kuyper heavily stressed the importance of Christian identity; he did not wish for Christians to sacrifice their faith when they participated in the various areas of the public realm.

In contrast to antithesis, common grace lays stress upon shared humanity and public responsibility. *Wisdom & Wonder* is a fresh, new and complete translation of two sections that Kuyper intended for his larger three-volume work on common grace. These sections were mistakenly omitted from the first edition of Kuyper's larger work. From 1895 to 1901 Kuyper wrote a series of articles in *De Heraut* that was later compiled and the three volumes were published in 1902, 1903, and 1904. "Common Grace in Science and Art," the sections translated here, first appeared as a separate bound volume in 1905 and were also added to later printings of the three-volume set.

What exactly is "common grace?" Kuyper articulated this doctrine as a development of earlier Reformed expressions of God's preserving work in the created order. This development was quite robust and much more expansive than statements of the doctrine in theologians such as John Calvin. Some of Kuyper's critics within Reformed circles saw this expansion as more inventive than developmental. Although Kuyper was not averse to grand statements and creative expression, common grace is far from a doctrinal innovation that veers off the tracks of faithfulness. Put simply, common grace responds to the question many have about our world: "How does the world go on after sin's entrance and how is it possible that 'good' things emerge from the hands of humans within and without a covenant relationship with God?" Common grace is God's restraint of the full effects of sin after the Fall, preservation and maintenance of the created order, and distribution of talents to human beings.

As a result of this merciful activity of God through the Holy Spirit's work in creation, it remains possible for humans to obey God's first commandment for stewardly dominion over the creation (see Gen. 1:28). This is not a saving, regenerating, or electing grace, but a preserving grace extended to the world God has made, and is seen in the human inclination to serve one's neighbor through work, pursue shalom in broken social situations, and defend equity in all forms of human interaction.

Wisdom & Wonder specifically addresses the domains of science and art. For Kuyper, science was not limited to "hard" sciences like chemistry and biology but also extended to the humanities and social sciences. Kuyper wrote at a time when it was an open question whether philosophy, literature, and theology could be considered properly "scientific." Here he expresses his view that science is intended to discover the deepest truth of all things, a truth that requires investigations that take us beyond surface-level encounters with various phenomena to the understanding of how all reality is an expression of the divine mind.

Similarly, when writing about art, Kuyper presents a view that begins with the link between religion and artistic expression and ultimately moves toward a statement on the proper independence of art from the domain of the church. Perhaps one of the most interesting features of Kuyper's discussion of art is his view that art, at its best, aims to express the final realization of God's glorious kingdom through media such as architecture, painting, and music. This does not mean that every artist consciously strives to create works approximating the consummated kingdom but that the desire to express the fullness of beauty tends to orient artists toward such a lofty goal.

Kuyper's focus on science and art resonates with contemporary discussions about Christian participation in both communities. At least since the time of Darwin, many Christians have perceived an often very real conflict with the world of science, and for those whose vocation brings them to research, teaching, or other science-related professions, there has been significant tension. Some have responded by abandoning the scientific mainstream in favor of a Christian alternative, while others have kept their faith and the work effectively separated, and still yet others have embraced an anti-intellectualism shrouded in a faith posture suspicious of any serious scientific research. Kuyper would encourage us to choose none of these paths; we should participate fully in the scientific domain, while aware of the fact that there will be a genuine antithesis between Christians and non-Christians at the level of ultimate explanation. For certain, Kuyper would encourage the embrace of all that falls under the domain of the sciences.

The domain of art is also an area of great challenge. From film to popular music to painting, Christian artists often occupy a domain that many perceive as draped with caution flags. There is a significant chasm between the world of art and the church, and those who regard themselves as dual citizens find themselves exasperated by the misunderstandings of their vocation within the church. As with science, there are many who tend to encourage limited participation in the arts or even withdrawal if the artist is not producing spiritually oriented works. Readers will see that Kuyper is aware of the pitfalls and promise of art while ultimately encouraging the pursuit of artistic expression in keeping with the image-bearing quality all humans embody as creators of beauty, value, wealth, and knowledge.

It is not necessary to have total agreement with a person in order to admire them or find their contributions to be of great value. Some of Kuyper's specific views on science and art may not be embraced by all readers; while incredibly prescient regarding some developments in society, Kuyper was not omniscient, and at times ventured opinions we might find surprising. This may be most apparent in the comments regarding Africans and "primitive peoples" that appear in these discussions of science and art. Like many of his era, Kuyper regarded Africans as far behind other civilized people groups. While his theology emphasized the creation of all humans in the divine image and while his emphasis on cultural diversity (multiformity) encourages humility about the extent of our knowledge, these emphases did not lead him to proper regard for all humans. While this reveals that Kuyper had feet of clay, this is no warrant for disregarding the tremendous contribution of works such as his volumes on common grace. Instead, this helps all of us to sharpen our critical thinking abilities; we can critique Kuyper on race and gender while also recognizing that such statements are in fact peripheral to his argument.

Abraham Kuyper's project on common grace is a welcome contribution to larger discussions about the role of Christians in society. In recent decades, some evangelicals in the United States have struggled to discern how to live with a robust faith and proper commitment to cultural, political, economic, and social engagement. For many, it seems as if the only options for Christian engagement are either some version of Christendom, which can appear to be an effort to run society according to the express dictates of Scripture, or a form of alternative witness, which is a kind of antithesis that emphasizes the practices of the Christian community as opposed to direct involvement in political or cultural domains.

Common grace helps us to see that other choices remain. God's sustaining work in creation encourages us to participate in the various areas of life, striving to discern the best ways to pursue education, art, politics, and business as we participate within these domains. Faithful Christian engagement means the pursuit of the fullness of human life in the totality of God's created order. This neither requires ecclesiastical sanction nor life as an alternate polis. For sure, every context will require us to see how to pursue faithfulness in different ways, but we can be encouraged that God by common grace has made it possible for us to participate in the public realm in multiple ways that contribute to the flourishing of the created order. *Wisdom & Wonder* is merely a taste of what Kuyper wrote on this great doctrine. May it whet your appetite.

PART ONE
SCIENCE

one

WISDOM

The advantage of knowledge is that wisdom
preserves the life of him who has it.
Ecclesiastes 7:12b

CR

IF WE ACKNOWLEDGE the contrast between the life of the state and society, then science definitely belongs to the sphere of societal life. Nevertheless this does not mitigate the fact that, as far as common grace is concerned, it could not have been included in our discussions concerning society. For whatever sets in motion societal activity originates in the intimate communal living of families in the same village or hamlet, in the same region or country. By contrast, although science as well as art must find the atmosphere for flourishing within that common life in society, nevertheless both derive their impulse from something that lies outside of society, from a unique motive. For this reason, science as well as art requires a separate treatment, and it is with the discussion of both of these that our exposition of common grace will conclude.*

First, then, let us emphasize the *independent character* of science. Before everything else it must be understood that science is a matter that stands on its own and may not be encumbered with any external chains. For that reason, if in its early stages science should still lack the strength to stand on its own legs, it can progress for a time being tied to the apron strings of others.

Wisdom & Wonder is a new and complete translation of two sections that were mistakenly omitted from the first edition of Kuyper's larger three-volume work on common grace, *De gemeene gratie*. These sections first appeared as *De gemeene gratie in wetenschap en kunst* (Amsterdam: Höveker & Wormser, 1905), and were added in later editions of the three-volume set.

Similarly, the free citizen living in the free state, who later would be keenly focused on independence, is, as a young child, initially carried by his nursemaid and learns to walk by holding on to her apron strings.

In this connection, people have shown how historically science could not have assumed its role initially without the help of the government and the church. Nevertheless, this observation supplies no proof at all against the independent character that belongs to science.

In every form of life, two stages may be distinguished. First is the stage of emergence followed by gradual growth, which continues until adulthood is reached. Only then does the second stage occur, when full-grown life is self-sufficient. This is why the gardener places a stick alongside a young plant and ties that plant to the stick. When, thanks to this support, the plant achieves full growth and is sufficiently rooted to be able to stand on its own strength, then the stick is removed and the plant stands by itself.

SCIENCE NEGLECTS ITS DIVINE CALLING IF IT PERMITS ITSELF AGAIN TO BECOME A SERVANT OF THE STATE OR THE CHURCH.

And that is how it went with science. In northern Europe, at any rate, science was planted and initially supported by the Christian church. Furthermore, science could have not survived without the support of the government. Nowadays, by contrast, science has become independent to the extent that it would far rather attempt to dominate church and state than continue being submissive to the domination of church and state. This independence belongs to science, and is not at all being usurped by science.

Science has not demanded such independence in overconfidence, but possesses this independence by divine design, so much so that science neglects its divine calling if it permits itself again to become a servant of the state or the church. Science is not a branch growing from the trunk of government service, and even less a branch that grows from the root of the church. Science possesses its own root, and science rests on this root. From this trunk that proceeds from this unique root, science must grow its branches and bear its fruit. As the well-known synodical report expressed it with such complete accuracy, science is "a unique creature of God," with its own principle of life, created to develop in conformity with that principle of life, that is, to develop in freedom.*

From this we can already observe that science belongs to *the creation*. Just think: if our human life had developed in its paradise situation, apart from sin, then science would have existed there just as it exists now, even though its development would obviously have been entirely different. Even though its character underwent a remarkable alteration as a consequence of sin, it may never be said that like the state and the church, science arose because of sin and thus from an intervening grace.

Without sin there would be no state, and apart from sin there would have been no Christian church, but there would have been science. To that extent, science is on the same level as marriage and family, both of which similarly have undergone significant alterations as a result of sin. But both of these, had sin never occurred, would have retained their independent existence even now, because they existed already in paradise. So just as marriage

---

*The synodical report that Kuyper mentions was written by his close friend and colleague Dr. Herman Bavinck, another major leader of the neo-Calvinist revival in the Netherlands. In the report Bavinck develops the idea of science (*wetenschap*) as a creation of God Almighty. For the full text of the report, see "Rapport van prof. dr. H. Bavinck over het rapport van deputaten voor de opleiding, voor zooveel handelend over het verband der kerken tot de Vrije Universiteit," in *Acta der generale synode van de Geformeerde Kerken in Nederland, gehouden te Middelburg, van 11 aug. tot sept. 1896* (Leiden: D. Donner, 1897), 125.

and family can hardly be said to owe their existence to the state or to the church, similarly science may not be construed as being dependent on either one of these. Science, too, arises from creation, and as such has received from the Creator a calling independent of the state and the church.

———

This independent position of science rests in the creation of humanity according to God's image. In the Lord our God exists an independent divine *thinking*, which did not arise within him from out of created things, but preceded the creation of all things. He does not think because he created, but he created after having thought.

This is what we confess in the doctrine of the divine decree. Although the manifestation of the will of God also lies within the decree, yet it was firmly fixed that this will of God was directed toward what he in his wisdom had conceptualized. A decree not preceded by any reflection cannot exist. This divine thinking that preceded his decree was not the appearing of random concepts that emerged from a mystical, unconscious undercurrent of his being, as some propose, but an altogether independent thinking, in the full divine clarity of consciousness. God was inspired by no one outside himself.

This is something that Holy Scripture expresses by saying that no one has instructed him, and no one has stood alongside him as counselor. The mind of the Lord is original with him. This is why Paul asks, "For who has known the mind of the Lord, or who has been his counselor?" (Rom. 11:34). Elsewhere he asks, "For who has understood the mind of the Lord so as to instruct him?" (1 Cor. 2:16). This thought had been formulated earlier by Isaiah with these words: "Who has measured the Spirit of the Lord, or what man shows him his counsel?" (Isa. 40:13). Accordingly it must certainly be confessed that the thinking was entirely independent and original in God, from which independent and original divine thinking proceeded the decree, and from this decree the world proceeded, just as even now all the history of the world likewise proceeds.

With majestic strokes Solomon sketches this same truth for us in the book of Proverbs, when he traces for us how wisdom was with God before any created thing proceeded from his hand. In the exalted language of Proverbs 8:22-31 this is revealed to us in these stanzas:

> The Lord possessed me [namely, wisdom] at the beginning of
>   his work,
>   the first of his acts of old.
> Ages ago I was set up,
>   at the first, before the beginning of the earth.
> When there were no depths I was brought forth,
>   when there were no springs abounding with water.
> Before the mountains had been shaped,
>   before the hills, I was brought forth,
> before he had made the earth with its fields,
>   or the first of the dust of the world.
> When he established the heavens, I was there;
>   when he drew a circle on the face of the deep,
> when he made firm the skies above,
>   when he established the fountains of the deep,
> when he assigned to the sea its limit,
>   so that the waters might not transgress his command,
> when he marked out the foundations of the earth,
>   then I was beside him, like a master workman,
> and I was daily his delight,
>   rejoicing before him always,
> rejoicing in his inhabited world
>   and delighting in the children of man.

In recalling this passage, John the evangelist teaches us that this wisdom in God was *the Word*, and that all things were created through that Word: "In the beginning was the Word, and the Word was with God, and the Word was God. He was in the beginning with God. All things were made through him, and without him was not anything made that was made. In him was life, and the life was the light of men" (John 1:1-4). The Greek phrase used for "the Word" is *ho logos*, and *logos* means *reason*. Because for us *reason* can be dormant until it comes to full clarity in the spoken word, this phrase is not translated, "In the beginning was *reason*," but, "In the beginning was *the Word*." This expresses that God's reason is to be pictured not as existing in a dormant state, only to come to clarity, but altogether differently, as being one with his being in full clarity from eternity to eternity.

Indeed, those churches that have continuously and jealously defended the doctrine of the decree have thereby zealously sought to guard the honor of God and the pure understanding of his divine essence. By contrast, the complaint may be registered that other churches, without denying the decree but nonetheless in fact permitting it to slip out of view and ignoring it, have granted entrance to an impure concept of the being of God. From this perspective it is rather mistaken, as people often construe the matter, to suggest that the conflict between the Reformed and Methodists and other parties has been waged merely about externalities.* Rather, that conflict touches the deepest point of religion itself, our confession regarding the being and the attributes of God.

---

*Kuyper's criticism here is not directly of individuals or churches within the Methodist-Wesleyan traditions, but of what he describes as "an unhealthy fruit" of the revival movement at the beginning of the nineteenth century, which set up a false tension between the subjectivity and individuality of spiritual life and the organic unity of a Christian worldview that addresses social, economic, political, and cultural questions.

If, therefore, God's thinking is primary, and if all of creation is to be understood simply as the outflow of that thinking of God, such that all things have come into existence and continue to exist through the Logos, that is, through divine reason, or more particularly, *through the Word*, then it must be the case that the divine thinking must be embedded in all created things. Thus there can be nothing in the universe that fails to express, to

THERE CAN BE NOTHING IN THE UNIVERSE THAT FAILS TO EXPRESS, TO INCARNATE, THE REVELATION OF THE THOUGHT OF GOD.

incarnate, the revelation of the thought of God. It was not the case that there existed an immeasurable mass of matter that God's thinking attempted to process, but rather divine thinking is embedded in all of creation. A thought of God constitutes the core of the essence of things, and it was primarily this thought of God that prescribes for created things their manner of existence, their form, their principle of life, their destiny, and their progress.

The whole creation is nothing but the visible curtain behind which radiates the exalted working of this divine thinking. Even as the child at play observes your pocket watch, and supposes it to be no more than a golden case and a dial with moving hands, so too the unreflective person observes in nature and in the entire creation nothing other than the external appearance of things. By contrast, you know better. You know that behind the watch's dial the hidden work of springs and gears occurs, and that the movement of the hands across the dial is caused by that hidden working. So too everyone instructed by the Word of God knows, in terms of God's creation, that behind that nature, behind that creation, a hidden, secret working of God's power and wisdom is occurring, and that only thereby do things operate as they do.

They know as well that this working is not an unconscious operation of a languidly propelled power, but the working of a power that is being led by *thinking*.

Now that thinking of God, which brings about the movement of all things in their course, is not working without plan or purpose or principle, but is rather a work directed to a purpose, moving toward that goal according to a fixed rule. This plan at its origin embedded within the creation everything indispensable for reaching that goal.

ALL THINGS HAVE PROCEEDED FROM THE THINKING OF GOD, FROM THE CONSCIOUSNESS OF GOD, FROM THE WORD OF GOD.

Consequently, all things have proceeded from the thinking of God, from the consciousness of God, from the Word of God. Thereby all things are sustained; to these all things owe their course of life and all things are guaranteed to meet their goal. So we can and must acknowledge and confess unconditionally that all of creation in its origin, existence, and progress constitutes one rich, integrated revelation of what God in eternity thought and established in his decree.

Now the only question is whether we human beings are gifted with a capacity to reflect that thinking of God.

It is absolutely clear that not every creature possesses that capacity. Even though the lily is clothed with a glory greater than that of Solomon in all his splendor, it knows nothing of its own beauty, and comprehends not the smallest bit of the thought of God that is expressed in its existence. No matter how magnificently the fish may live in the water, the fish knows nothing of the composition of the water, of the capacity that the water has to keep a body afloat, or of the nourishing properties contained in the water. It is even evident that the animals endowed with developed instincts, such as the ant, the bee, the spider, and the like, neither understand anything of what they do, nor do they comprehend anything of what God is revealing in them.

To be sure, we must always use great caution in expressing ourselves regarding the animals, since we cannot penetrate their inner existence. But we may and must say this much, that with animals we observe nothing of ongoing development, and that nothing is revealed to us about a higher aptitude or a higher consciousness that was supposedly bestowed on the animals.

We know a bit more about angels (taking into account the devils as fallen angels). But regarding angels it is written that they desire to see into things they do not understand. No matter how much knowledge angels may have, in certain respects they continue to stand below us.

By contrast, concerning a human being this great truth is revealed, namely, that every human being is created according to the image of God. On this basis the Reformed churches confess that the original man in his nature, that is, by virtue of his creation, not through supernatural grace but according to the creation order, had received holiness, righteousness, and *wisdom*. Here, then, attention is drawn to a capacity bestowed upon human beings enabling them to pry loose from its shell, as it were, the thought of God that lies embedded and embodied in the creation, and to grasp it in such a way that from the creation they could reflect the thought which God had embodied in that creation when he created it.

This capacity of human nature was not added as something extra, but belongs to the foundation of human nature itself.

In this way, then, we obtain three truths that fit together. First, the full and rich clarity of God's thoughts existed in God from eternity. Second, in the creation God has revealed, embedded, and embodied a rich fullness of his thoughts. And third, God created in human beings, as his image-bearers, the capacity to understand, to grasp, to reflect, and to arrange within a totality these thoughts expressed in the creation.

The essence of human science rests on these three realities.

Such a magnificent capacity was not given to human beings for them to keep it unused. They must apply this capacity bestowed upon them for the purpose for which it was given. The moment human beings employ this capacity for reflecting the thoughts of God from the creation, science arises. And to the extent that human beings do this more precisely and more diligently, human science will possess greater stability and richer content.

———

Nevertheless, one should not understand this to mean that this task of science in itself, in its full range, was being assigned to every human being. That cannot be. The range of this task is far too great for that, and the capacity of the individual person is too limited.

The principal confession of the creation of human beings according to God's image reaches much farther than the acknowledgment that we personally and individually, each for oneself, belong to God's race. Rather, it comes into its own only when we extend it to our entire race down through the ages, and in the combination of the talents bestowed upon all the various persons. It is not so that merely one individual brain, or one individual genius, or one individual talent has been equipped to understand the fullness of the Word in creation, but all of them together have the goal of making this apprehension possible among people. Had it been intended otherwise, then every person, man or woman, would have to be in full possession of all genius and all talent. But this is not the case. Genius and talent appear only as distributed among a few individuals. We readily accept the claim that, in this respect, on account of sin, much has changed from what would have been apart from sin. Even so, no one would argue that according to the original creation ordinance no difference, no distinction would have existed between people.

Even the starry heavens do not disclose to us an infinite number of stars identical to each other, but stars in infinite constellations which all differ from each other. Precisely in this multiform differentiation the splendor of the firmament radiates. Similarly, one should not suppose that in the world of humanity God intended noth-

WE MAY DRAW NO OTHER CONCLUSION THAN THAT THE RICH VARIETY AMONG PEOPLE, IN TERMS OF APTITUDE AND TALENT, CAME FORTH FROM THE CREATION ITSELF AND BELONGS TO THE ESSENCE OF HUMAN NATURE.

ing else than monotone uniformity, and that multiformity and variety arose for the first time through sin. If that were so, then sin would have enriched rather than impoverished life.

Moreover, the mere fact that God created a *man* and a *woman* proves indisputably that identical uniformity was not part of the plan of creation. So we may draw no other conclusion than that the rich variety among people, in terms of aptitude and talent, came forth from the creation itself and belongs to the essence of human nature. If this is so, then it follows automatically that in relation to the image of God, no single human being bears this feature of God in its fullness, but that all talent and all genius together comprise the capacity for incorporating within itself this fullness of the thought of God.

Science is thus constructed not on the basis of what one person observes, discovers, imagines, and organizes into one system in his or her thinking. Rather, science arises from the fruit of the thinking, imagining, and reflecting of successive generations in the course of centuries, and by means of the cooperation of everyone. Each person does indeed possess individual knowledge, that is, the fragmented knowledge that a person acquires. But God's creation is so unspeakably immense, and the richness of thoughts that lie embedded in his creation is so immeasurably deep, that the fragmented knowledge of any one person virtually disappears. That little fragment is also science in the most general sense of the word. But it is not *the* science that operates as a unique creature of God with its own life principle in order to fulfill a unique task.

ANYONE FAMILIAR WITH THE ARENA OF SCIENCE ANTICIPATES WITH JOY THE PROGRESS IN THE SPHERE OF SCIENCE THAT IS TO BE EXPECTED IN THIS TWENTIETH CENTURY.

Science in this exalted sense originates only through the cooperation of many people. It advances only gradually in the generations that come on the scene, and thus only gradually acquires that stability and that rich content that guarantee it an independent existence, and begins to appear only in this more general form as an influence in life.

At the same time, from this it follows directly that science can acquire significance only with the passing of centuries, and will be able to develop in its richest fullness only at the end of time. Science is a mighty temple whose foundations had to be dug first, and then its foundation had to be set. Only then could its walls be erected on that foundation, and its battlements could be built once the walls were finished. This temple can display the full splendor of its architecture, its colors, and its shapes only when *the entire building is completed*. This explains why centuries have passed when, among a number of nations, there was hardly any science to speak of in the higher sense. In our country as well one would have searched in vain for science in that sense among the Batavians.* This also explains why only the history of recent centuries,

---

*The Batavians were an ancient Germanic tribe native to the Netherlands.

especially of the sixteenth and nineteenth centuries, narrates for us the story of such a mighty flourishing of science. Finally, this also helps explain what we all sense, namely, how even today science stands at the beginning of its great accomplishments; and why anyone familiar with the arena of science anticipates with joy the progress in the sphere of science that is to be expected in this twentieth century.

Science is not the personally acquired possession of each person, but gradually increased in significance and stability only as the fruit of the work of many people, among many nations, in the course of centuries.

From this fact proceeds the independent character of science. For science does not come into existence by first having one of the best architects produce a fully developed blueprint for the building of this temple, and then having subsequent generations labor quietly by common consent according to that original blueprint, in order eventually to build the temple.

Rather, the entire temple is constructed *without* a human blueprint and *without* human agreement. It seems to arise by itself. Each one quarries his own little stone and brings it forward to have it cemented into the building. Then comes another person who removes that stone, refashions it, and lays it differently. Working separately from one another, without any mutual agreement and without the least bit of direction from other people, with everybody milling about, everyone going his own way, each person constructs science as he thinks right.

Through that endless confusion, it nevertheless appears that, in the course of centuries, out of this apparently confused labor, a temple emerges, displaying the stability of architecture, manifesting style, and already generating speculation about how the entire building will ever be completed.

At that point, then, it must be acknowledged and confessed that all this labor was led and directed unseen by an Architect and Artisan whom no one saw. At this point it will not do to suggest that this most beautiful result emerged by accident, without plan, all by itself. Rather, we must confess that God himself developed his own divine plan for this construction, created the geniuses and talents for implementing that plan, and directed the labor of everyone and made them fruitful so that what he wanted and still wants would indeed become reality.

Seen this way, however, science is then also an invention of God, which he called into being, causing it to travel its paths of development in the manner he himself had ordained for it.

This means nothing else except to say and to confess with gratitude that God himself called science into being as his creature, and accordingly that science occupies its own independent place in our human life.

two

KNOWLEDGE

The fear of the Lord is the beginning of knowledge.
Proverbs 1:7a

CR

WE HAVE DISCOVERED that original thought existed in God. A manifestation and embodiment of this original thinking appears to us in the created universe and to human beings a capacity has been given for reflecting on and investigating this divine thinking in a uniquely human manner. This reflection proceeds fragmentarily, but with the help of competent direction and organization nevertheless does result in a system of knowledge. This system of human reflection constitutes science which is a unique creature of God, with a calling to independently fulfill a task assigned to it by God himself. God has organized science in this way for the magnifying of his holy name.

In this way, and in no other way, the light of God's Word discloses the foundation. The truth expressed here is understood even more deeply through Holy Scripture, and is inferred from the unique being, life, and work of God by means of the amazing disclosure that Wisdom or the Word possessed personal eternal existence in God, and is truly God himself.

At this point we need not discuss that deeper background, however, since we are not at the moment discussing the original, i.e., archetypal, knowledge in God, but rather the reflected, or ectypal, knowledge that arises under God's arrangement within and from human consciousness.

As an aside, to prevent misunderstanding we must pay explicit attention to a uniqueness of Holy Scripture. As we read Holy Scripture, we repeatedly get the impression that instead of commending knowledge or being wise, the Bible more often condemns human knowledge. As we read in Isaiah, "Your wisdom and your knowledge led you astray" (Isa. 47:10). Or as the Preacher says, "He who increases knowledge increases sorrow" (Eccles. 1:18). Or as Paul writes to the Corinthians, "For the wisdom of this world is folly with God" (1 Cor. 3:19).

WE CAN EASILY UNDERSTAND WHY NOT A FEW PEOPLE VIEW SCIENCE AS A HOSTILE POWER THAT SHOULD SOONER BE COMBATED THAN CULTIVATED.

These statements, together with numerous others, sooner discourage us from receiving what the world calls knowledge, rather than fill us with respect for human knowledge. Couple this with the mocking tone with which people of science almost systematically speak about the revelation of Scripture and about things that for us are holy. And let us not ignore the destruction of many people's faith brought about by the so-called results of science. When one puts all of this together, then it can easily be explained why a particular suspicion toward science has crept in among believers. We can easily understand why not a few people view science as a hostile power that should sooner be combated than cultivated. And we can readily comprehend, finally, why some people curse knowledge and therefore prefer to retreat to the safety of their own tents.

In response to this, we will mention only that Scripture distinguishes between *true* and *false* knowledge. On the one hand, Scripture testifies that "the advantage of knowledge is that wisdom preserves the life of him who has it" (Eccles. 7:12). On the other hand, however, Scripture also warns us against "what is falsely called 'knowledge'" (1 Tim. 6:20). In this way, Scripture sets a knowledge that is *excellent* over against a knowledge that is *falsely* called such. Keeping that distinction in view enables us to understand why on the one hand Scripture warns us against that false knowledge, and on the other hand Scripture attempts to inspire love and respect for true knowledge.

———

This distinction arose because of sin. Sin is what lures and tempts people to place science outside of a relationship with God, thereby stealing science from God, and ultimately turning science against God. The flower of true science possesses its root in the fear of the Lord, grows forth from the fear of the Lord, and finds in that fear of the Lord its principle, its motive, its starting point. If through sin a person is cut off from this root that proceeds from the fear of the Lord, the inevitable result must be that such a person will present as science something that is a facade without any essence.

Nevertheless, we must be alert for one particular misunderstanding. Some identify this contrast in such a way that the good science, the true science, the "science of the saints," as it is called elsewhere, exists exclusively in the knowledge of God's grace in Christ.* This construal suggests that false knowledge refers to investigating the things of the world. But this is incorrect. There can be a *false* knowledge of both holy things and worldly things. Conversely, there can be both *true* knowledge of the sacred revelation

———

*In his work *The Way of Salvation and Perfection*, Roman Catholic bishop and saint Alphonsus Maria de Liguori (1696-1787) contrasted sacred and profane learning. In a reflection titled "The Science of the Saints," he wrote, "Blessed is he who has received from God the science of the saints. The science of the saints is to know the love of God. How many in the world are well versed in literature, in mathematics, in foreign and ancient languages! But what will all this profit them, if they know not the love of God?" The phrase "science of the saints" also alludes more generally to Proverbs 9:10: "The fear of the LORD is the beginning of wisdom, and the knowledge of the Holy One is insight." See Alphonsus de Liguori, *The Complete Works of St. Alphonsus de Liguori,* vol. 2, ed. Eugene Grimm (New York: Benzinger Bros, 1886), 189.

of Scripture, as well as true knowledge in relation to the life of the world. In both instances, both with the false knowledge and with the true knowledge, the object of science is and remains the totality of everything that can be known by us as human beings.

The distinction between the true science and the false science lies not in the arena where people perform their investigations, but in the manner with which they investigate, and in the principle from which people begin to investigate. Sin has not only corrupted our moral life, but has also darkened our understanding. The result can only be that anyone attempting to reach scientific knowledge with that darkened understanding is bound to acquire a distorted view of things, and thereby reach false conclusions.

So this darkening of human understanding by sin has led science down the wrong path. We cannot help but remain exposed to this danger, as long as this darkening of human understanding receives no counterweight in the illumination of that understanding by the Holy Spirit.

Apart from common grace, the decline of science would have become absolute without that illumination by the Holy Spirit. Left to itself, sin progresses from bad to worse. Sin makes you slide down a slope on which no one can remain standing.

Anyone who ignores common grace can come to no other conclusion than that all science done outside the arena of the holy lives off appearance and delusion, and necessarily results in misleading anyone listening to its voice. Yet the outcome shows that this is not the case. Among the Greeks, who were completely deprived of the light of Scripture, a science arose that continues to amaze us with the many beautiful and true things it offers us. The names of Socrates, Plato, and Aristotle have always been esteemed among Christian thinkers. It is no exaggeration to insist that the thinking of Aristotle has been one of the most powerful instruments leading Christians themselves to still deeper reflection. In modern times as well, no one can deny that in the disciplines of astronomy, botany, zoology, physics, and so on, a rich science is blossoming. Although being conducted almost exclusively by people who are strangers to the fear of the Lord, this science has nevertheless produced a treasury of knowledge that we as Christians admire and gratefully use.

ALTHOUGH SIN DOES INDEED SPREAD ITS CORRUPTION, NEVERTHELESS COMMON GRACE HAS INTERVENED IN ORDER TO TEMPER AND RESTRAIN THIS OPERATION OF SIN.

Consequently, we are confronting the fact that outside Christian circles a science has blossomed that, seen from one angle, supplied us with genuine and true knowledge and yet, seen from another angle, has led to a philosophy of life and a worldview that run directly contrary to the truth of God's Word. Or, to state it differently, we are really confronting a science that has arisen from the world, a science that lies very definitely under the dominion of sin and that nevertheless, on the other hand, may boast of results from which sin's darkening is virtually absent. We can explain this only by saying that although sin does indeed spread its corruption, nevertheless common grace has intervened in order to temper and restrain this operation of sin.

Also as far as science is concerned, the situation we find is explicable only if we give *both* of these their due, on the one hand, the darkening of our understanding by sin, and on the other hand, God's common grace that has placed a limitation on this darkening. That we very definitely may and must speak in this regard of God's activity is immediately evident from the undeniable fact that in people like Plato and Aristotle, Kant and Darwin, stars of the first order have shined, geniuses of the highest caliber, people who expressed very profound ideas, even though they were not professing Christians. They did not have this genius from themselves, but received their talent from God who created them and equipped them for their intellectual labor.

———————

In order to see this, we must not suffice with the general slogan, "darkening by sin," but must account for how this darkening works. Has sin resulted in our inability any longer to think logically? Has sin induced in us an inability to perceive what exists and occurs around us? Does sin place a blindfold over our eyes so that we no longer see or observe? Absolutely not. Whenever you discuss anything with another person, you repeatedly presuppose both for yourself and for your discussion partner the capacity for logical thought. You do not hesitate for a moment, wondering whether what you are seeing or hearing exists as you have perceived it. As a rule you live life with a complete feeling of certainty. We have not ceased on account of sin to be rational creatures. And when we compare our own existence with that of the animals, we are completely conscious of the superiority that we enjoy as human beings, thanks to our human reason. The power that we have gradually acquired over the animals and over the whole earth is then so plain and real that such power clearly convinces us of the genuineness of our research and thinking.

Therefore, it cannot be denied that the darkening through sin is observable here as well. How utterly weak is the power of logical thinking among many people! How numerous are the mistakes and errors in our reasoning into which we have repeatedly fallen! How often does not sloth creep in and permeate research at its deepest level! How much study occurs for the sake of examinations or for a career, lacking the motivation of sacred enthusiasm for the subject!

But even though we admit all of this, all of this is still no more than a partial defect, and not a darkening that *impedes* our seeing.

No, the actual darkening of sin lies in something else entirely.

Sin's darkening lies in this, that we lost the gift of grasping the true context, the proper coherence, the systematic integration of all things. Now we view everything only externally, not in its core and essence, each thing individually but not in their mutual connection and in their origin from God. That connection, that coherence of things in their original connection with God, can be sensed only in our spirit. It does not lie in things outside of us, and therefore could be known and reflected upon only to the extent that our spirit lived in vital relationship with God, and was able to trace this coherence of divine thoughts proceeding from God.

> SIN'S DARKENING LIES IN THIS, THAT WE LOST THE GIFT OF GRASPING THE TRUE CONTEXT, THE PROPER COHERENCE, THE SYSTEMATIC INTEGRATION OF ALL THINGS.

Our human spirit possessed precisely that characteristic at its perfect creation, but lost exactly that characteristic when sin severed the vital connection uniting us with God. Just like a dog or a bird sees a palace with stones and wood and mortar, and perhaps color, but neither comprehends nor understands anything of the building's architecture or style, nor the purpose of its rooms and windows, so we stand with darkened understanding before the temple of creation. We see the parts, pieces, and elements, but we no longer have an eye for the style of this temple. We can no longer guess its architect, and so we can no longer understand this temple of creation in its unity, origin, and destiny. We are like an architect bereft of his senses who at one time, when he was in his right mind, grasped and perceived the entire building in its coherence, but who now peeks out of his cell window to stare blankly at walls and pinnacles without any longer understanding the style of the building.

Blind to God and to divine things—this means not only that we who now dwell in the darkening of our sin can no longer rise to God, but also that we are no longer in a position to perceive in creation the coherence of God's thoughts. This means that we are unable to perceive the wholeness of the creation, and unable to form a clear concept of the plan of that creation. Consequently, we are unable to arrive at a true knowledge of that creation.

We can certainly acquire correct knowledge about stone and wood and paint and metal, but we can no longer arrive at a correct view of the style, the fundamental idea, the theme, and the goal of this building called creation. Surely science does not consist simply in examining wood and stone and metal, but an investigation most properly and essentially becomes science when it succeeds in capturing a mirror image of the whole. Precisely for that reason the darkening of sin obstructs the acquisition not of the knowledge of the details but knowledge in its more exalted and nobler sense.

As long as you look at creation while excluding human beings and discounting God, science still conjures up wonders by its precise dissecting of things and tracing the laws governing their motion. But no sooner do you take humans into account than you arrive at spiritual questions that bring you into contact with the center of all spiritual life, namely, with God. At this moment, all certainty vanishes, as one school of scientific opinion stands alongside another, as one paradigm opposes another, until at last pervasive despair overcomes the researchers. Their knowledge advances, of course, as long as they are studying the human body and can observe anything of the human psyche that comes to physical expression, but the moment they enter the characteristically *spiritual* arena, the outcome is speculation and assumption, with one theory displacing another theory, leading finally to doubt and skepticism.

How this has all come about would become far clearer still if we knew more about the original situation when our human race had proceeded from the hand of its Creator and had not yet been affected by sin. We do not know very much about this situation. Nevertheless, from several pieces of helpful information we can deduce sufficient knowledge relevant for comprehending the difference that entered creation through sin.

In our current situation we can arrive at the knowledge of things only by observation and analysis. But that is not how it was in paradise. For we read that God brought the animals to Adam, and that when he first saw them, Adam immediately perceived the nature of these animals in such a way that he immediately gave them names (Gen. 2:18-20). Naturally this cannot mean that when each animal paraded past him, Adam simply uttered a sound that had no sense or meaning. Imagine that someone carried two- or three-hundred suitcases past you, and that when you saw each of these suitcases, one after the other, you invented a sound, without purpose or sense. Long before the hundredth suitcase came by, you would have forgotten the name you had given the first one.

What purpose was served by Adam naming the animals? Eve was not there yet. No one heard him. This story makes sense, then, only if you realize that Adam immediately perceived the nature of each animal, and expressed his insight into the animal's nature by giving it a name corresponding to its nature.

Now, if Adam enjoyed this position with respect to the animal world, there is no reason for denying that he enjoyed a similar position with respect to the plant world, indeed, to the entire natural world. We no longer possess that characteristic, that capacity immediately to perceive and understand the essence of plants and animals. If we want to learn to understand a plant or an animal, then we must observe that animal and that plant carefully for a long time, and from what we observe gradually draw conclusions about their nature. This occurs apart from us ever learning to understand their essence. Even their instincts still remain a completely unsolved riddle for us.

But Adam possessed this capacity. Taking this into account, we will understand as well how Adam would have arrived almost immediately at a knowledge of the entire creation if sin had not intervened. This knowledge would have led to a direct understanding of the entire creation in the context of its origin and its destiny.

There is something else. Adam not only perceived the essence of things, but he also named them. This naming is something that no longer exists for us. We can certainly give a name to a foreign object, but we either take such a name from another people, like the Dutch borrow English terms for rails, trams, and locomotives, or we construct such a name with the aid of Greek words, like telegraph, telephone, electricity, and so on. But we can invent new names in our own language to express the essence of things only by means of linguistic composition or by adopting words already in use. We can no longer create language.

Adam, by contrast, could do this. For him the *concept* of a thing existed together with the *essence* of a thing, and the *word* existed in an organic connection with this *concept*. Adam was never taught to speak by his mother, but he spoke automatically, and what God spoke to him, which he must have understood, already shows how highly developed his conceptual and linguistic capacities were. So we are not exaggerating when we claim that in his own thoughts and consciousness, Adam possessed a clarity, insight, and unity that we have lost.

Apart from sin, science would have taken an entirely different path, and would have been constructed with an immediacy that we can scarcely imagine. What is meant by the darkening of understanding through sin becomes evident to us in the right way only when we deduce from this what Adam could do and what we can no longer do. Science was an immediate possession for Adam, but for us science is bread we can taste in no other way than in the sweat of our spirits, by means of difficult and strenuous labor.

Although in that manner science has acquired an entirely different character as a consequence of sin, such that our science is now the fruit of arduous industry, precise observation, careful analysis, and conscientious synthesis, nevertheless what existed formerly was not entirely lost.

The instincts of animals demonstrate how intuitively both precise knowledge and exact actions can occur apart from prior study or practice.

The spider weaves its web and the bee builds its honeycomb with a precision and certainty that are unsurpassable by any kind of human construction. Take, for example, a young spider that never saw a web, and you will nonetheless see that quite soon it is spinning and weaving a web that is just as artistic and proficient. We should mention in this connection that the apostle Paul observes concerning our human knowledge that it is now only partial, and that it now operates with mirror images, but at a later time it will become entirely different and will then be characterized as perfect.* Now, however, we no longer possess that kind of knowledge, nor the capacity to acquire such knowledge. Now everything comes through observation, through learning, through practice, through study.

Nevertheless, there is something in human experience that lies between instinct and acquired knowledge, a kind of mediated knowledge that Holy Scripture everywhere sets forth by the

---

*See 1 Corinthians 13:8-12.

term *wisdom*. We know simply from practical experience that this is something other than *scientific knowledge*. Time and again we meet among the simplest people the kind of individual who is gifted with extraordinarily practical wisdom. Such individuals do not have very much academic learning. Occasionally some of them cannot even read or write, and yet, when it comes to giving advice, to deciding, or to acting, they can speak so *wisely*, and they know how to act so *wisely*, that they always succeed and put to shame people who are more expert than they.

As a general rule, a woman is less formally educated than a man, but how often do we not see that the wife of a learned man possesses much wiser insight into human experience than he, embarrassing her husband with all his knowledge? Such *wisdom* you will find in the East, but also in the West. Solomon had never studied at what we call university, and most likely had not taken any exams, and yet people came from every region in the East to hear Solomon's *wisdom*. Even though a special inspiration came into play here, nevertheless among other peoples of the East, stories circulated about such wise people who were actually gifted with an extremely clear and lucid insight into matters.

Such wisdom is one of the precious elements in the life of a society. People have been surprised occasionally by the high degree of practical wisdom manifested by individuals even among primitive tribes. In the most complete sense this is not comparable to an animal's instinct. Nor is it any longer the immediate knowledge that Adam possessed. Yet it recalls both, and has something in common with both. The similarity is that apparently apart from any effort, such knowledge feels comfortable dealing with the context of things, and with sure and firm grasp knows how to choose what is correct. It is as though such wise people are following a higher leading that equips them always to find what is correct. They always hit the target.

What is being revealed here is nothing other than the operation of common grace, which has preserved some remnant of paradise and enriches our life, even life affected by sin.

That this same trait has also developed sinfully in the craftiness of deceit and in the cunning of the deceiver is obvious.

But that happens with *every* gift supplied by common grace. It endeavors to enrich us but at the same time runs the risk of being abused. Hushai and Ahithophel are examples of both.* Nevertheless, in our sinful situation science did not arise from this wisdom.

WHAT IS BEING REVEALED HERE IS NOTHING OTHER THAN THE OPERATION OF COMMON GRACE, WHICH HAS PRESERVED SOME REMNANT OF PARADISE AND ENRICHES OUR LIFE, EVEN LIFE AFFECTED BY SIN.

Wisdom is useful for the moment or for practical living, but it does not construct knowledge of the whole. For that reason, common grace supplies a second element. Once bereft of immediate insight into the essence of things, the pathway was opened so that through the indefatigable labor of further research, observation, analysis, imagination, and reflection, a person can acquire at least some knowledge of the external side of things and can learn to understand the appearance of things together, even if not the law of their motion.

It is this second gift proceeding from common grace that down through the centuries has led to the appearance of what we now call science. Only through this means can human beings, as much as in them lies, attain science. What special grace contributes to this we will consider in the following chapter.

---

*See 2 Samuel 17:1-24.

three

UNDERSTANDING

For who knows a person's thoughts except the spirit of that person, which is in him? So also no one comprehends the thoughts of God except the Spirit of God.

1 Corinthians 2:11

֍

SIN HAS CAUSED a certain darkening of our understanding. As a result, the clarity of our human science suffers appreciably in terms of that understanding. This would not be so bad if our knowledge rested entirely and exclusively on *observation* or arose by way of *experience*. Then we would possess in our consciousness nothing other than a mirror, which would reflect the world around us. It is true that a mirror without a crack is preferable. Nevertheless a cracked mirror can assist if necessary.

Therefore, we can postulate that the mirror of our consciousness became cracked by sin, and the reflection of the world on that cracked surface would provide us with a knowledge of the world that is not altogether incorrect. Some injury to the unity of the image would occur, but you would be able to observe the parts of the image of the world very well.

Precisely here, however, lurks the difficulty. Within us there is something entirely different than a reflecting mirror. That which casts its reflection on the mirror of our consciousness is absolutely not the only phenomenon that exists that leads us to doing science. Our consciousness, our reason, and our understanding are something altogether different from a camera. Our understanding does include a photographic capacity, but this performs limited assistance for the essential operation of our scientific thinking.

This is analogous to seeing with our eye. In the lens of our eyes there is, if you will, a camera. It captures an image; another person can even observe that captured reflection in our eye. But our *seeing* is a far more complex activity. You can discover something like this most easily when you compare a person who is looking intently with another one who is staring thoughtlessly, both of whose glances capture the same ship, the same house, or whatever. The lens of each person's eye has the same reflection and yet the one person sees it while the other does not. This is sufficient proof that there is a duality in every essential *seeing*. First, there is the reflection of something on the lens of our eye; second, our minds engage what is reflected.

The same is true of our intellectual knowledge. Manifold observation captures the image, but with that capturing of the image the activity of our intellect is hardly finished. In fact, at that point the higher work of our mind is only beginning.

This contrast between capturing the reflected image of things and the higher work of our mind requires some further explanation. An observation can be simple and composite; it can be direct and peripheral. If before my eyes I see cattle grazing in the pasture, those animals are to be observed directly in terms of their appearance and their movement. No professor of zoology is needed for that; a farm boy can do it just as well.

By contrast, in order to determine whether an infectious microbe is lurking in the lung, what microbes they might be, and the damage those microbes might do, a far more complex and analytical observation is needed, which can be performed only by an expert in that field. The lung is not exposed and the microbes are too small. Even though such observation requires far more effort, and even though it cannot occur without using various helpful tools, and various kinds of deductive knowledge must be taken into account in connection with all of this, nevertheless what we have here is and remains nothing more than *observation*.

One can call such complex, diffuse, intensive, and analytical observation *science*, but basically it still lies entirely on the same continuum as ordinary, direct observation. It is far more refined; it requires incomparably higher talent; it demands far more serious effort from us; but the result remains one and the same. With the naked eye the farm boy sees the cattle grazing in the field, he counts them, he distinguishes their color, he sees them walking and moving about. The researcher follows the same route to discover the microbes in that diseased lung, to count them, to distinguish them in terms of their form, and to identify their movement.

All higher science begins with the evaluation of things, but its actual task consists in processing what it has observed and drawing conclusions from that. From making many observations higher science proceeds to compose a complex theory that clearly explains the relevant causes, operative principles, and interconnectedness of phenomena. If this description is true, then there can be no dispute about whether those independent observations provide the material for higher science, although they do not yet constitute that science itself.

In opposition to this, however, in the preceding century people became more and more accustomed to supposing that such artificial observation already constituted the actual science, and from this premise they ascribed the highest scientific character to those disciplines occupied with the observation *of nature*. To this the French gave the honorable title of *sciènces exactes* (natural sciences), and the British give them the still shorter title of *sciences*, as if by themselves these studies could claim the honorable title of science.

———————

This attitude may have been caused by the carelessness, even disregard, with which observation was treated in times past. But in this position lurk an error and a danger that demand a protest.

Behind this position lies an attempt to free science from our subjectivity or, if you please, from our person. Science is supposed to be neutral, and in order to be neutral, science must be disconnected from our personal being. Only that should qualify as science which everyone assented to immediately or agreed to on the basis of demonstration. That is what people meant by insisting that science had to be impartial, and that with science our only concern had to be to find truth.

But in this way the issue was falsified. Why a researcher would ever search for anything but the truth is inconceivable in the scientific arena. Yes, one can have a further goal in view.

The doctor studying a diseased lung hopes to cure it, and the miner who examines a mine wants to find gold. But both that doctor and that miner are engaged first and foremost in searching for *truth*. How else would the lung be healed? Could a mine yield gold that was not there? Everyone agrees, then, that in the first phase of the scientific endeavor—that of *proper observation*—truth remains the chief goal. Since we do not produce the object to be observed but find it outside of ourselves, the very nature of the task requires us to aim for as great an objectivity in observation as possible, in which process our own ego should play as passive a role as possible.

This remark, which is proper in itself, has given rise to the proposal that we accept as science only what is observed in that manner by everyone alike and only what can be concluded directly from the data. The subjective personality of the scientist, his own ego, was allowed no voice, and the old concept that our mind is a *tabula rasa*, a blank sheet of paper, surfaced in new form. Our mind itself had no content. We were simply recording devices, elegant photographic cameras, nothing more.

While this approach is applied in physics and chemistry, it went wrong when people carried it over to history, philosophy, or any other human science. Indeed, as soon as there was talk of a science of anthropology, people were so kind as to deny all these higher disciplines a genuinely scientific character and to reserve that for those fields which only measure, weigh, and count. This has pushed people within the spiritual sciences to base their work as much as possible on external observation. Even what we call psychology had to be constructed entirely on outward appearances. This has led to the increasing materializing of *all* science, feeding the false notion that spiritual life arose from material causes. And this trend, generally speaking, has won the field as the dominant feature of modern science.

> THE INDEPENDENT CHARACTER OF THE SPIRITUAL WITHIN US MAY NOT BE STRIPPED AWAY, OR WE WILL END UP DIRECTLY DENYING THE SPIRIT IN GENERAL AND DENYING GOD.

This we must oppose. The independent character of the spiritual within us may not be stripped away, or we will end up directly denying the spirit in general and denying God.

If the independence of the spiritual life, of the spirit, and so also of the Father of spirits, is to remain intact, then science has to reckon with that independent factor of the mind, and do so as much in the person who is researching as in the spiritual things researched. From this the conclusion follows that the claim is absurd which argues that "only that is scientific which can be proven to the consent of all." Were all persons doing science alike, the statement would undoubtedly be true. But since persons doing science are *not* alike, since different points of departure prevail from one consciousness to another, and since not only *differences* but *contradictions* arise time and again, as a result the illusion of a single science can no longer be maintained.

Our observation of the spiritual world can begin in no other way than with the consultation of our own spirit. Only from our own spirit do we come to some knowledge of the spiritual existence of others. Seeing and hearing, weighing and measuring can merely help in this, but do nothing more. If we had no human spirit, whatever we see and hear of others would never have brought us to discover the spiritual being within them. "For who knows a person's thoughts," says Scripture, "except the spirit of that person, which is in him?" (1 Cor. 2:11). So it is indeed. Self-consciousness is the means whereby we come to know the human spirit in general.

Nor is that all. If a spiritual world exists in distinction from the material world, then genuine fellowship with that spiritual world is possible for us only through our own spirit. What we observe of the operation of God's Spirit in nature, of the human spirit in history, in our surroundings, and in literature undoubtedly helps to enrich our knowledge. But experience teaches us every day that all of this does not lead to a correct knowledge of God or man. We must possess an internal spirit that brings us into contact with this realm of spiritual life.

THINKING ITSELF IS A SPIRITUAL ACTIVITY.

We should not rely primarily on outward observation and when we can go no further, and only then call on our own spirit for help. That is cowardice. No, we must boldly maintain the two-fold nature of the terrain of investigation. On the one hand, there is a terrain of external things, where everything depends on seeing and hearing, weighing and measuring. On the other hand, there is a terrain of invisible, spiritual things, where our own internal spirit deserves the right of first action and where the outwardly observable *can* and *may* function only as a servant.

We will sense how deeply this penetrates the essence of science when we consider that science without reflection is unimaginable. *Thinking* itself is a spiritual activity. The very instrument that serves as a trowel in the construction of the edifice of science belongs not to the external but to the invisible. The law governing this thinking can never be discovered through hearing, seeing, measuring, or weighing, but manifests itself in the human spirit. The contradiction arises immediately that our thinking cannot help but inquire about the *origin*, the *coherence*, and the *destiny* of things, whereas observation neither can nor does teach us anything about these.

Observation cannot commence before something exists. Suppose for a moment that you were present at creation; you still would have seen nothing with your eye nor heard anything with your ear before it came into being, and you could not have said anything about the cause that brought it about. Likewise, it is impossible for us to come by way of observation or calculation to a fixed comprehensive conclusion about the *coherence* of things.

Through careful observation we may notice one thing or another. We discover connections between various things. We also observe how one thing triggers another. But even in this respect our knowledge is so limited that we continually encounter insoluble riddles. We are not satisfied if we are able to discern a particular connection between things. Our higher consciousness demands that this connection be explained by means of a *rational* system, so that we can perceive how everything fits together and what purpose that system serves.

We see, for example, that there is a connection between Gladstone's death, the collapse of the liberal party in England, the discovery of the gold mines in the Rand, the Rhodes clique, and the war in Transvaal.* This is not difficult. But that does not sat-

---

*Kuyper is pointing to the seemingly isolated connection between events that took place in England, such as the death of Prime Minister Gladstone in 1898, which contributed to instability and disagreement among the leadership of the

isfy us, and all of Europe and America are unpleasantly affected by this brutal course of events, resenting the fact that there is no power to end it.

We want to know not only the causal connection, but the spirit within us does not rest until we also understand the idea that caused this connection to develop. Our sense of justice will not allow itself to be lulled to sleep, and we remain restless until we can clarify the relationship of justice in terms of this connection between things.

Now this depends on the third point that we mentioned, the *destiny* of things. Our mind finds no rest in the concept of an endless continuation of our life here on earth. Personally, we cannot imagine having lived during all the ages this world has already existed. Even less can we imagine that century after century the carpenter should do nothing but saw and plane his wood, or that the sailor would drift age after age from port to port. Everything must come to an end, and we cannot help but imagine that this entire world must come to an end. Then what? Could everything that ever existed have had no other purpose than to perish? So the idea arises that an ultimate goal, a destination must have been established for all things, and that everything that was or is must be oriented toward reaching that goal, that destination.

But because it only hears, sees, measures, and weighs, science can tell us nothing about that, because it cannot see past the end.

Liberal party and the discovery of large deposits of gold in the Witwatersrand in the Transvaal region (Johannesburg) of South Africa during the latter half of the nineteenth century. Transvaal was an independent state settled by the Boers in the Dutch emigration to South Africa, and the Rhodes clique refers to the British High Commission's plot to overthrow Paul Kruger, the president of the Transvaal Republic, which led to the Second Anglo-Boer War (1899-1902). This war, in turn, led to a change in approach to foreign policy from Britain, which now set about looking for more allies.

To the extent that science clings to the visible and the observable, it cannot even entertain the question of the origin, coherence, and destiny of things. The theory of evolution imagines that it can do this now with respect to origins, but this is nothing less than self-deception, for it traces things back to the first atoms and the energy they contained, but of the origin of these atoms and energy it can tell us nothing. It thus shifts the question without answering it.

> THE THEORY OF EVOLUTION IMAGINES THAT IT CAN DO THIS NOW WITH RESPECT TO ORIGINS, BUT THIS IS NOTHING LESS THAN SELF-DECEPTION, FOR IT TRACES THINGS BACK TO THE FIRST ATOMS AND THE ENERGY THEY CONTAINED, BUT OF THE ORIGIN OF THESE ATOMS AND ENERGY IT CAN TELL US NOTHING.

Nonetheless, our mind constantly and repeatedly poses those three great and immense problems, challenges from which the mind *cannot* free itself, three principial questions about which the spirit within us always muses again and again: From where? How? And to what end? The mighty rise of Darwinism is itself in no small part to be explained in terms of unreflective people imagining that here at least was sufficient answer to the first of these three questions.

Anyone following what we have written thus far concerning science will have no trouble forming a clear picture of the state of the question. Because the natural sciences can measure and weigh with precision, they can offer a kind of certainty that is easily demonstrable to everyone. This claim led to the insistence that science refers only to what ultimately garners the agreement of everyone. This was followed with the effort to separate science from the person, the subject doing science, and to orient science as much as was feasible toward the sensate-observable side.

Having been drawn into this view, the spiritual sciences retreated as far as was feasible to that position where the spiritual manifests itself in the visible. They were, as they put it, applying the method of the natural sciences to the spiritual sciences. In this way, with respect to the spiritual, the independence of its own existence was contested. There was no soul any longer; there was no God any longer. There was nothing more than matter and manifestations of matter. This resulted in the complete materialization of all science. This is the main feature that characterizes all of modern science.

So it does not help to say, "I would not go that far. I have my faith, and for that faith I rely on Holy Scripture." For as long as you nonetheless continue holding to the false view of modern science, you either remain on the horns of a dilemma or your scientific labor continually pulls you toward the dismantling of the spiritual.

What must happen at this point is you must break in principle with this entire view of science. Before everything else, the independence of the spirit, of spiritual life, and of the law governing that spiritual life must be established for you. You must perceive and acknowledge that your *thinking* also belongs to that spiritual life. You must see clearly that because of this, the researching person cannot remain satisfied with observing, measuring, and weighing. The spirit within you irresistibly confronts you with entirely different problems. These are problems that no set of scales, no plumb bob can solve, because these problems involve an arena where observation is impossible.

So you must embrace the conclusion that observation may not degrade your spirit to the status of assistant. Rather the spirit within you must employ the observation of visible things as an assistant in order to further regulate the investigation performed by science.

Of course, from the beginning of creation the invisible things of God were understood from the creation, both his eternal power and his deity (Rom. 1:20). Whereas the lion also has an eye, and the eagle has a still sharper eye than you, and both observe the creatures you see, they cannot understand them nor can they surmise anything of the eternal power and the divinity of the Lord of Lords, simply because they lack a spirit, and thus they lack the very idea of a God.

You, by contrast, seeing these same creatures, do understand from them the eternal power and divinity of the Lord. This understanding comes to you not from those creatures, but rather because you are created with the human spirit within you, and because at creation the human spirit included the idea, the notion, the consciousness of God's existence.

YOU MAY POINT OUT THAT ANY NUMBER OF PEOPLE OBSERVE THE SAME CREATURES YET ARE NOT MOVED TO WORSHIP GOD'S ETERNAL POWER AND DIVINITY. TO WHICH WE ANSWER THAT SEEING THROUGH A MICROSCOPE DEPENDS UPON ITS BEING PROPERLY SET UP AND FOCUSED.

You may point out that any number of people observe the same creatures yet are not moved to worship God's eternal power and divinity. To which we answer that seeing through a microscope depends upon its being properly set up and focused. Anybody who has ever worked with a high-power microscope knows how much trouble it takes to see what you need to see.

So too here, you may not consider man as he is now in his false position. In this respect you need to begin with man as God created him. Through nature the first man saw God in his eternal power and divinity in a way that our eye will not and cannot behold him. We have no right to complain that we see so little. If I focus the microscope for a student and he changes the lens or the adjustment so that he sees nothing, the blame for not being able to see is his, not mine. This is exactly what we did when we fell into sin. Having no right to complain, we should rather be grateful that it pleased God to help us in this helpless situation by readjusting the microscope through common grace so that we can at least see *something*, even if not with the former clarity.

But we can sin against this grace too. If someone is so totally engrossed in the sensory world, such that the idea of God more and more fades from his soul, if someone closets himself within his self-sufficient thinking so that he places God outside his field of vision, then it only stands to reason that he is like an eagle that sees more sharply than common folk but, for all his eagle eye, can no longer discern the living God in his creation.

Yet this is no cause for self-congratulation. If you discern a glimmer of divine life in creatures, this is but grace imparted to you. This is a grace that makes you no better but, on the contrary, should cause you to thank him all the more humbly for condescending to reveal his divine presence in your spirit, thereby enriching your life so immeasurably.

four
SIN

For it is written, "I will destroy the wisdom of the wise, and
the discernment of the discerning I will thwart."
Where is the one who is wise? Where is the scribe?
Where is the debater of this age? Has not God
made foolish the wisdom of the world?
1 Corinthians 1:19-20

CR

NEGLECTING ALREADY at one's starting point to maintain the independence of the *spirit* from *matter* will eventually lead one, by the time the destination is reached, from worshiping man ultimately to idolizing the material. Applying the scientific method to the higher sciences makes it impossible to maintain the independence of the spirit. Any science choosing this route will wander farther and farther away from God, and will finally deny him entirely.

In this connection, the scientific researcher who takes his starting point in the world around him, and stakes his honor on grasping for neutral objectivity, is doomed by his very method to seeing the independent existence of his own ego finally perish. This is why we are insisting so vigorously that the subjective starting point once again be honored in science.

Modern science is dominated by distrust when it comes to our own deepest sense of life, and that distrust is nothing but unbelief. What people lose thereby they attempt to recover by locating their fulcrum in the consciousness of the prevailing majority. Whatever is generally regarded as true in scientific circles people will dare to accept for themselves.

What people generally agree upon in this manner is called *the* truth, the truth that people profess to honor. Pressed a bit further, they sense that such a general agreement constitutes no proof at all, so they suppose that only what I can make so clear to all persons of sound mind and sufficient education such that they finally understand and agree with it belongs to what is scientifically established. The Germans especially have made this their hobby, by inventing the term *universally valid** to describe this. This term refers to only what is observable, what is ultimately unable to be contradicted, and that for which one can logically compel agreement from every logically thinking person.

At the same time, however, this means that the thinker with the most impoverished sense has framed the case, since he has denied all the richer content of the human consciousness while validating as truth only what he has agreed with. This is like an army moving under orders that the cavalry not advance any faster than the infantry, nor the infantry any faster than its slowest soldier. Even though within this position faith is indispensable for progress (no matter that it was no more than believing in one single axiom), nevertheless the outcome was that everyone who possessed richer faith ultimately had to go along with and adapt to the researcher with the least faith. From this it follows that all Christian researchers who allowed themselves to be pulled in this direction were required to place the far richer content of their own conscious faith outside the scientific domain, or even to surrender their faith or drift toward apostasy.

For that reason, Christian thinkers became more convinced of the need to restore to his proper place the person who does science. Only in this way could the possibility emerge for maintaining the independence of spirit from matter, and thus also the existence of God in science. They increasingly saw this to be the position of Holy Scripture as well. After all, Scripture knows nothing of this high-minded *universal validity*, as if truth referred only to what everybody ultimately had agreed upon. On the contrary, Holy Scripture declared clearly that the wisdom and knowledge that the world derives from its own principles stand directly opposed

allgemeingültig

to true science. Scripture establishes as sharply as possible that the difference between the knowledge of the world, which is foolishness to God, and the true knowledge that is valid for God, arises from the difference within the spirit in the investigating subject.

There are two kinds of people. Scripture calls them "natural" and "spiritual," and says this of them in 1 Corinthians 2:11-15:

> For who knows a person's thoughts except the spirit of that person, which is in him? So also no one comprehends the thoughts of God except the Spirit of God. Now we have received not the spirit of the world, but the Spirit who is from God, that we might understand the things freely given us by God. And we impart this in words not taught by human wisdom but taught by the Spirit, interpreting spiritual truths to those who are spiritual. The natural person does not accept the things of the Spirit of God, for they are folly to him, and he is not able to understand them because they are spiritually discerned. The spiritual person judges all things, but is himself to be judged by no one.

Naturally this does not mean that there is not a lower kind of science that circumvents this antithesis. To the extent that results are governed by factual observation, obtained by weighing and measuring and counting, all scientific researchers are equal. As soon as people move above this lower kind of science, however, to higher forms of science, at that point the personal subject makes a contribution, in terms of which the difference between the "natural" man and the "spiritual" man comes into play. This phenomenon is definitely not restricted to the science of theology, but is present in every spiritual science, including the philosophical framework for the natural sciences.

———

From this premise it must follow that investigators part into two camps on the level of higher science. What the one calls *wis-*

dom, Scripture—along with every Christian—calls *foolishness*; conversely, the knowledge of the world laughs at what we call science, and thinks *foolishness* is too weak a word for expressing its derision for our science. Other than by surrendering the antithesis set forth by Scripture, how can people argue from a Christian standpoint that our science and the world's science must be one? How can we escape the division of the scientific enterprise into two well-defined groups? How then can we escape the principle that the distinction operative here arises from the differing predispositions of the personal subjects, as one lives from the awareness and consciousness of the unregenerate world, while the other lives from the renewing of our spirit that only radical regeneration brings about?

It is clear that with its antithesis between a "natural" man and a "spiritual" man, Scripture is not merely referring to a person who does and another who does not take Holy Scripture into account. Its pronouncement goes much deeper by positing the distinction between having and not having received the Spirit of God. It states so emphatically, "We have received not *the spirit of the world*, but *the Spirit who is from God*" (1 Cor. 2:12). This corresponds entirely with what Jesus himself said, that "unless one is born of water and the Spirit, he *cannot enter the kingdom of God*" (John 3:5). If you agree that the kingdom of God is definitely not identical to the institutional church, but rules our entire world-and-life view, then Jesus' declaration means that only one who has received the inner illumination of the Holy Spirit is in a position to obtain such a perspective on the whole of things, one that corresponds to the truth and essence of things.

If it is established that there are two kinds of people who differ in principle in their ego and in their inner consciousness, then the scientific inquiry of each cannot proceed hand in hand. They cannot work together building the same wall. Each must build for himself. Inevitably a twofold kind of science must arise in parallel, on the one hand, the science of those taking their starting point in the spirit of the world, and on the other hand, the science of those taking their starting point in the Spirit who is from God. Since this difference among people arises through regeneration, which in the New Testament is called *palingenesis*, people have distinguished this twofold kind of science posited over against each other as the science of palingenesis and the science that is pursued apart from palingenesis.

Thus if the fundamental difference lies in the personal subject, in terms of whether one is regenerate or unregenerate, then it is just as true that a second fundamental difference corresponds to this, in terms of whether in connection with scientific research one does or does not take into account God's special revelation as that has been preserved and sealed for us in Holy Scripture. We placed the working of the Spirit of God within the personal subject in the foreground only because numerous researchers busy themselves with Holy Scripture but they lack the inner illumination of the Spirit. They first water down the content of Holy Scripture, and then they interpret it in conformity with the spirit of the world. When finally they see that this does not work, they dispute all of the authority and content of Holy Scripture, unraveling and destroying it.

By itself Scripture cannot help us make progress in this respect. Precisely because Holy Scripture is not of the world, but its content was brought into the world by God's grace, it can be neither comprehended nor understood unless the one teaching it has been stirred and enlightened by the Spirit of God. Merely saying, "I take account of Scripture," never leads to a satisfactory result unless account is also taken of what is needed for the correct understanding of Scripture. The operation of God's Spirit within the investigating subject must be paired at this point with the objective operation of the Spirit in special revelation. Precisely at this point special revelation shines its light in common grace, in order to strengthen it.

ONLY THE REVELATION OF HOLY SCRIPTURE SUPPLIES CERTAINTY REGARDING THE CARDINAL ISSUES THAT DOMINATE OUR ENTIRE VIEW OF LIFE, AND YET IT WILL NOT DO TO SAY THAT THESE ISSUES BELONG TO THE DOMAIN OF PARTICULAR GRACE.

It is undeniable that throughout the ages, common grace has been operative among numerous more developed peoples, in order to advance to a high degree the spiritual development in our human race by creating intellectual geniuses and bestowing brilliant talents. Nevertheless, it was only special revelation that shed such indispensable light upon the weightiest issues, especially those involving the origin, government, and destiny of all things. Only the revelation of Holy Scripture supplies certainty regarding the cardinal issues that dominate our entire view of life, and yet it will not do to say that these issues belong to the domain of particular grace.

Particular grace is that grace which saves a sinner and which therefore extends only to the elect. By contrast, Holy Scripture discloses to us the mystique of the creation, reveals to us the ordinance of God's providence in the Noahic covenant, and warns us that this world is heading toward a final catastrophe. All of this definitely affects not only the elect, but all people and every living thing, including the animals, even as the animals were purposely included in the Noahic covenant. It states emphatically, "Behold, I establish my covenant with you and your offspring after you, and *with every living creature that is with you, the birds, the livestock, and every beast of the earth with you, as many as came out of the ark; it is for every beast of the earth*" (Gen. 9:9-10). How could this belong under particular grace?

So, too, when the Psalmist in Psalm 104 portrays the life of the animals, and when the prophet Isaiah portrays the life of the farmer, how could all of this be assigned to particular grace simply because we find it in the Bible? People sense that this does not fit. It is perfectly true that this revelation concerning the deepest issues of life, along with this more accurate perspective concerning nature, has reached us along the route of special revelation, and would not have been granted to us if there had been no particular grace. All this notwithstanding, it is perfectly clear that these themselves constitute no part or portion of particular grace. Rather, they are a strengthening of the light of common grace, a strengthening that comes to us from special revelation.

It is of the highest importance, however, that we place clearly in the foreground the fact that this strengthening came from special revelation. Had it been the case that special revelation restricted itself to only what, strictly speaking, concerns the salvation of the sinner, and ignored all the rest, we would lack the requisite data for building a temple of science that rested on a Christian foundation. One would have been able to get nothing more than religious doctrine, something Egeling termed, "the way of salvation."* We would not attain even a complete theology. But this is *not* what Scripture does. It not only gives us the direction for the way of salvation, but it also sheds light around us concerning the great problems of the world.

Still more, Scripture does not arrange both of those—the way of salvation and natural life—like two ticket windows next to each other, but continually weaves them together like threads, giving us a view of the world, its origin, its course within his-

---

*Lucas Egeling (1764-1835) was a Leiden pastor who wrote a two-volume work entitled *The Way of Salvation According to Biblical Standards*, or *De weg der zaligheid naar het beloop des Bijbels*, 2 vols. (Amsterdam: C. Covens, 1820-1822).

tory, and its ultimate destiny, within which, as though within an invisible framework, the entire work of salvation occurs. In this way, with these fixed points before us, we are afforded the possibility for constructing an entire Christian approach to science that liberates us from idle speculation and provides us knowledge concerning the real state of things, that is, concerning reality as it was, is, and shall be.

Without the personal subject coming under scrutiny, no difference in insight would be conceivable in terms of the scientific results of scientific investigation conducted on the basis of Scripture. As long as they thought logically, every Christian would have to reach entirely identical conclusions, and no difference of conviction could exist among Christians in the scientific arena.

But as the results teach us every day, this is not the case. It is true at a certain level, but as soon as people move from the root to the top of the stalk of this plant, it is no longer the case. This should not strike us as strange, if we take into account the significance of the personal subject, as we have recently shown to be necessary. This difference of insight could be reduced to a minimum only if the same divine authority that is inherent in revelation continued in an infallible manner to regulate our interpretation of Holy Scripture. The Roman church believes in the existence of such a continuing authority, and has thereby succeeded in no small measure in nurturing unity of conviction.

Yet we should not overestimate this. For even in the domain of the Roman Catholic Church, it is hardly the case that every investigative result is automatically governed by the pronouncement of ecclesiastical authority. With regard to numerous subordinate matters, Roman Catholic investigators reach quite divergent results. But this difference is naturally far greater among us Protestants who do not recognize such a continuing divine authority given to the church, and who believe in the leading of the Holy Spirit. But we know such leading of the Holy Spirit in no other way than as it is interwoven in the struggles of the personal subjects. For us, that leading is not uniform, that is, moving to the same outcome for everyone. Rather, this leading progresses through the contest of opinions and in this way displays the single rich truth in a multiplicity of ideas and convictions.

In itself that multiformity contains nothing injurious. Rather, it should be viewed in no other way such that even apart from sin, the splendor of the truth would have been able to shine most brightly simply in that variegation of convictions.

What is injurious in this are only the *antitheses* that have arisen, whose origin could lie nowhere else than in the outworking of sin.

The colors that exist when the beam of light shines through the prism are multiform, but together they constitute a harmonious ray. There is difference, but no antithesis at all.

Therefore, one can assume only that apart from sin, a rich variety of opinion and conviction would have existed, and that only through the sin that continues to work in creation have our variegations arisen so sharply over against one another that they have generated, in part at least, absolute antitheses. Everyone must struggle continually to maintain the variegations, but also to clarify what operates as an antithesis, and to be sensitive about cultivating harmony.

On the one hand, controversy is waged so that the differences might not be erased. But on the other hand, peace is sought in order to hold on to the unity. The unity automatically appears in the light, as soon as the enmity of the world's science shifts the battle to those deepest principles and to the very foundation of our communal life. At that point, people see time and again how those who stood sharply opposed to each other when it came to evaluating derivative postulates, suddenly join hands when it comes to defending the communal foundation.

We stand opposed to each other regarding the view of the image of God and original righteousness. But no sooner does the theory of evolution issue its claim that human beings were made according to the image of the animal, and even came from the animal itself, than Roman Catholics, Greek Orthodox, Lutherans, Anabaptists, and Reformed all join hands with new vigor to defend the creation of human beings according to God's image.

So amid diversity there remains a certain unity to be maintained, and history teaches us how a twofold process occurs in sequence. When the urge for unity went too far, so that it threatened to turn the necessary heterogeneity into uniformity, there came a period when the unity was virtually forgotten and by means of intense struggle, the diversity of the multiform reality once again received its due. But when people forgot that unity and emphasized the diversity so sharply that finally only antitheses survived, then an entirely new period arose when the attack on the commonly shared foundations became so intense that the need to do justice again to the shared roots automatically evidenced itself in every sphere.

During the Middle Ages, the diversity was sacrificed for unity. During the Reformation, diversity reared its head so high that often unity was no longer considered. During the eighteenth and the first half of the nineteenth centuries, appreciation for diversity succumbed to the indifference of superficiality. Since then, diversity has again gained ground, but just when that diversity was about to destroy the catholicity of the church, along came the theory of evolution, which is forcing us once again to place more emphasis on unity.

The exchange of ideas that the Christian life underwent in those different periods altered nothing with regard to the existence of certain ineradicable natural distinctions, because in principle they are closely related to the different capacities among people, nations, and times, the better to grasp the single revealed truth from this or that side. This explains why we are not in a position to grasp the truth comprehensively. In proportion to our capacities for comprehension, and to the extent that this capacity for comprehension develops in certain circumstances and under various external influences, to that extent the same truth is seen, grasped, and expressed differently by one people than by another.

Even in our little Europe, the makeup of spirits is different in the east than in the west, and different again in the south and in the north. The fact that the south remained Roman Catholic, the east remained Greek Orthodox, and that in the north the Lutheran lifestyle took root, while in the west it was the Reformed lifestyle that developed, is no accident, but is related to differences in ancestry, differences of history, differences in disposition, together with differences in mental and spiritual fervor. They have all accepted the same identical Christianity, but Christianity made different impressions on everyone. Each group assimilated Christianity in its own way, and after assimilating it, each attempts in distinctive ways to manifest Christianity in their worship and to concretize the Christian faith in living.

The distinction between the four main ecclesiastical traditions just mentioned should therefore not be explained on the basis of chance or arbitrariness, but originates in a difference of spiritual and societal disposition, which operated psychologically to lead inevitably to these four different foundations.

These four main varieties are analogous to plants. The one plant flourishes better in one country, another flourishes better in a different country. You can transplant them in different soil, but the outcome shows that the soil will yield the best result if you allow the plant to grow where it belongs.

The same is true here. There are Roman Catholics and Lutherans in Russia, just like there are Reformed people in Denmark, and Lutherans in Italy, even as there are Lutherans and Roman Catholics in the Netherlands and in England. But even so, the main stream in all these countries has continued to flow throughout the centuries in the same direction. In each of these countries, Christianity manifests itself most powerfully in the form that corresponds to the nature and disposition of the people. There exists here a natural connection between what the Christian religion finds in the national character and the form which the Christian religion takes. The greater the aptitude of a people, the purer that form will be. The less developed the people are, the more disappointing that form will be.

We find the claim to be incontrovertible that our national resilience reached its most magnificent expression once our people had discovered the so-called Reformed or Calvinist expression of life within the Christian religion. From this, one may deduce that a necessary connection exists between the character of our people and Calvinism, and that the latter fits the former. For that reason, it was definitely a mistake when people in the eighteenth and nineteenth centuries considered the Calvinist form of Christian living to be something short-lived, good for the past but useless for us, leading them to seek their well-being in a more general Protestantism.

This resulted in people importing a theology into the Netherlands from Germany, one that was Lutheran in its underlying idea, one that found no adequate soil here and thus could never thrive here. The outcome has also shown how this exotic plant, despite its rapid growth, nevertheless did not succeed. Meanwhile the Reformed manner of faith and life had hardly begun to show itself once again when it received acclamation from many quarters, and has already at this time restored to us an original, indigenous Dutch theology. Calvinism is the plant that, by virtue of disposition and history, belongs here. As soon as this plant once again spreads its roots here, people will continue to see its stalks shoot up quickly, with foliage that is verdant and with fruit that is healthy and abundant.

five

EDUCATION

In [Christ] are hidden all the treasures
of wisdom and knowledge.
Colossians 2:3

CR

SCRIPTURE SAYS that "the wisdom of this world is folly with God" (1 Cor. 3:19). This does not mean, as everyone senses, that to the extent that science rejects special revelation, it would not expand and validate our dominion over nature in various respects.

Rather, quite differently, this means that science fails as soon as it attempts to penetrate from the observable to the spiritual background of reality, and from the acquired data proceeds to attempt to build an entire construct. It puts forth with great fanfare what appears in God's light to be foolishness, that is, in conflict with essentiality and reality.

Everything comes down to ensuring that God's complete independence from the world is confessed, and also ensuring that the independence of spirit from matter is resolutely maintained. To that end, resistance is mounted against the inclination to subject the spiritual sciences to the method of the natural sciences.

Should this resistance succeed, immediately the difference that exists between one person and another would necessarily assert itself, a difference involving the extent to which a person continues to be wholly ensnared in the darkening of sin, thus rejecting God's special revelation. Or, as a regenerated person, one manages to peer through the darkness by means of conversion and of empathizing with the revelation of God's Word.

That spiritual light within the soul and that lamp for the feet that are provided in God's Word bring all Christians to the same basic perspective, but not yet to uniformity in thought and conduct. Their subjectivity is not a fixed replica of the same model, but displays diversity. No two original thinkers think exactly identically. Within these variegations, however, four main lines emerge, one of which is Calvinism, which for anyone who is Reformed is the most correct.

This leads among Christians, then, to four ways of envisioning the world and life. One who aims in his scientific labor to produce an integrated structure rather than a mosaic will build steadily according to the lines he acknowledges to be the most correct.

This explains why the Roman Catholic structure will be different than the scientific structure we acquire. As a consequence, precisely because it seeks the truth above everything else, all higher science must lead each thinker to join together with what his fellow thinkers have constructed and continue to construct in his own generation.

For that reason, we must reject as ineffective every attempt to build in the spiritual sciences, as well as in the higher science generally, together with all who reject special revelation. The same goes for building together with those who, even though they accept this revelation, nonetheless by virtue of their differently oriented subjectivity build in a style that is not ours and cannot be ours without violating our past and our own subjectivity.

———

From this it follows that all investigators can work together in those studies done outside subjective differences, but they must separate and go their own ways as soon as their study focuses on the spiritual sciences and on the higher scientific summary of the totality. With regard to those latter studies, believers and nonbelievers must go their separate ways.

Often they can certainly exchange the benefits of the results of one another's investigation, but they cannot labor together in building a temple of science. Much less may believers retreat to their ecclesiastical corner and, satisfied with simply having faith, abandon the building of the temple of science to unbelievers, as though science does not concern them. This they may not do, because the scientific enterprise is not an exercise in human pride but rather a duty God has laid upon us.

God's honor requires the human spirit to probe the entire complexity of what has been created, in order to discover God's majesty and wisdom and to express those in human thoughts with human language. Since the unbelieving world can do nothing but obscure God's majesty and wisdom, Christian thinkers are called to put their shoulders to that grand task that they alone can perform even if it were to bear no benefit for their own lives.

MUCH LESS MAY BELIEVERS RETREAT TO THEIR ECCLESIASTICAL CORNER AND, SATISFIED WITH SIMPLY HAVING FAITH, ABANDON THE BUILDING OF THE TEMPLE OF SCIENCE TO UNBELIEVERS, AS THOUGH SCIENCE DOES NOT CONCERN THEM. THIS THEY MAY NOT DO, BECAUSE THE SCIENTIFIC ENTERPRISE IS NOT AN EXERCISE IN HUMAN PRIDE BUT RATHER A DUTY GOD HAS LAID UPON US.

Fortunately, the latter is not the case. On the contrary, only when Christian science leads us to place ourselves within a clearly considered and lucidly explicated perspective of the world and of life does the thinking Christian come to have a view of things that corresponds to his faith, supporting and strengthening rather than undermining it.

After all, it is obvious that as it lives in the midst of this world, confessing Christianity cannot suffice with its faith-confession, but like every human being, the Christian also needs a certain understanding of the world in which he dwells. If for this he receives no guidance from a Christian perspective, then he can and will have no choice but to adopt the results of unbelieving science. In so doing, he lives with a world-and-life view that does not fit his faith, but one that irreconcilably contradicts his confession at numerous points. This then results in experiencing schizophrenia in his thinking, whereby the content of his confession and the scientific perspective in which he labors come to exist irreconcilably alongside each other. That destroys the unity of his thinking, and also weakens his power. The inevitable result is that gradually his faith begins to yield to his scientific view, and without noticing it, he slips into the unbelieving mode of viewing the world. In the nineteenth century this resulted in the rise of a mixed mode of viewing the world that, similar to the Ethicals in our own country, sought to unite several parts of faith with several parts of unbelieving philosophy into one entity that always remains a hybrid.*

Conversely, our duty is that we who confess Jesus Christ take hold of science as an instrument for propagating our faith-conviction. We have seen repeatedly how a group of believers who do not sense this obligation isolates itself from surrounding society, retreating to a separate corner, maintaining their position usually among the less developed social classes, losing all influence on the course of events and on the formation of public opinion.

In the nature of the case, the general mentality among the populace receives its imprint from the academics. The universities stipulate the direction of thought for people of influence. From the universities this mode of thinking is reproduced among politicians, lawyers, physicians, teachers, and writers. By means of such influence that mode of thinking is carried over into the press,

---

*After his conversion in the early 1860s, Kuyper came to see the danger that theological modernism posed to vibrant Christian faith. In this respect, he was especially critical of the modernist Ethical theology of Friedrich Schleiermacher and Albrecht Ritschl. A great danger of Ethical theology was its pantheist impulse to "blur the boundaries" between God and creature.

to secondary and elementary schools, and to the network of our bureaucratic officials.

If that university life and the influence it produces on the populace remain exclusively in the hands of unbelievers, then public opinion will ultimately be turned entirely in that direction, also morally and religiously, and will have a most injurious effect in our Christian circles as well.

IN THE NATURE OF THE CASE, THE GENERAL MENTALITY AMONG THE POPULACE RECEIVES ITS IMPRINT FROM THE ACADEMICS.

There is only one means for preventing this, one that requires Christian thinkers to establish a university-level movement, and by means of that academic movement manifest a different mode of perceiving and thinking, reproducing it among people who pursue these university studies. The eventual result would be a cadre of people who were intellectually developed to exercise influence among the populace, people who could enter the field of public discourse.

The life of particular grace does not stand by itself, but has been placed by God amid the life of common grace. Since Holy Scripture is definitely not limited to opening up for us the way of salvation, but has been given also to enrich common grace with new light, for those who confess that Word not to make this higher light to shine upon the arena of science, which belongs to the field of common grace, constitutes deficient devotion to duty.

A person is hardly inclined to imagine that this practice of science envisions the world of thought exclusively. Even though it is absolutely true that the reflection of God's thoughts from the creation upon the mirror of our human consciousness is required simply for the honor of God's name, nevertheless this more re-fined knowledge does not reside beyond the realm of daily living.

In the ordination of God's common grace, science is also one of the most powerful means for combating sin together with the error and misery flowing from sin. Science practiced in the Lord's name functions as an antidote to the poison of sin, but not as if science would ever possess the power to effect the transition of any person's soul from death unto life. The instrument that God has ordained for that kind of transition is faith, and this saving faith can arise only from the re-creation of a person's soul, namely, from regeneration, which God himself imparts within the secrecy of the soul without us and without any instrument. For that rea-son, science does not belong to particular grace, nor can it belong there, but occupies its own place in that glorious work of common grace that restrains sin, error, and misery in their manifestations.

To be convinced of this, one need only compare human life like that found among the dark-skinned tribes of Africa with the life lived by people in our European countries, where the torch of science has shined its light for a long time. The ravages of supersti-tion, including those that still appear among us only sporadically, continue to dominate all of life in Africa. One can scarcely speak of a system of jurisprudence worthy of that name, whereby order and rule in human society could be introduced among those tribes. No one has ever heard of the freedoms and rights of the people replacing the arbitrariness of tribal chieftains. Women endure lives of denigration and humiliation. There is no concept of nur-turing children in any refined sense. People lack every capacity to resist the ravaging power of nature. Diseases and epidemics leave destruction in their path, with no thought given to any hygienic measures. Care for the poor or the needy does not exist there. A higher development of the spirit is entirely unknown there; people do not even know how to read. The notions of honesty and fidelity have sunk very low. Human life has no value and is not respected. And the most scandalous sensuousness dominates there without shame and without restraint.

Now it also happens that in our European countries every sin of this nature lingers in secret. It is also the case that our refined, unnatural manner of living has brought about new miseries that people formerly never experienced. But despite this, it is undeniable that public human society among us bears a far nobler and elevated character, not only among Christians but among unbelievers as well. That this is due to common grace we unfolded earlier in great detail, and need not be repeated here. But in this context the remarkable contribution made by science to this elevation of public life needs to be mentioned. Superstition cannot survive where the light of science shines.*

The science of jurisprudence has been the great instrument for establishing order and rule in society, for restraining violence, and by creating safety for persons and property, for resisting the outbreak of destruction arising from passion. Medical science may have gone awry in many ways, but to it still belongs the honor that in God's hands it has been the instrument for relieving much suffering, for curbing many diseases, and for disarming much latent evil before its outbreak. Natural science has armed us in extraordinary ways against the destructive power of nature, and has subjected that nature to our dominion. The science of the humanities has affected our human thinking in a way that is wonderfully illuminating and influential. The science of theology has been the instrument ordained by God for setting straight

---

*Kuyper's attitude of cultural superiority and triumphalism manifest here and in other places in this text is in sharp contrast to his own stated convictions regarding the basic equality of all human beings. For more on the problematic aspects of Kuyper's perspective on indigenous peoples, including expressions most today would find to be distasteful, see Vincent E. Bacote's introduction, page 28.

the basic concepts of our thinking, those essential principles from which healthy human living can arise, for making its root spread and for sharpening the vision that had to choose between truth and error.

It is indeed true that many of these benefits have not been correctly processed by science, and much more has been accomplished by civil servants, judges, advocates, physicians, health professionals, engineers, and so on. But this takes nothing away from the significance of science, since it was science that formed and equipped these people, after all.

This power that lies embedded within science for resisting sin, error, and misery was perceived during the Middle Ages so clearly that it was not unusual during that period to view the practice of science nearly exclusively from that perspective, to which even the division of science into various disciplines is undoubtedly related. The discipline of theology had to combat error, that of jurisprudence had to combat violence and dishonesty, the health sciences had to fight sickness and diseases, while the natural sciences had to combat the destructive power of nature. This perspective naturally did not do justice to the disciplines of the humanities, since at that point they had not won for themselves an independent place but rather served merely as formative training for the other disciplines.

If you view science from that perspective, then the danger lurking at hand is evident should the study within these various disciplines be cut off from its firm basis in the truth of God. For the discipline of theology this requires no separate explanation, because the history of our homeland as well has demonstrated in an all too sorry way how the science of theology, once it is cut loose from the authority of God's Word, ceases to be an instrument for combating error, and instead becomes an instrument to spread error anew and causes it to be spread in continually novel forms. The same appears to obtain, however, for the discipline of jurisprudence as well. Once it departs from the security that justice possesses only in God and his Word, practitioners of jurisprudence are able to deduce justice from no other source than tradition and society's sense of justice. And since this sense of justice is as unstable as the waters of a flowing stream, it steadily undermines the security of the concept of justice. Hereby not only is our entire civic and judicial life disturbed and jeopardized, but civic justice has also lost its firm footing, and even penal justice is brought to the point of abandoning its high calling as penal justice, to the point of destroying every concept of guilt with the slogan of no accountability.

No further argument is required to see that the discipline of medicine yields profound danger if it proceeds in the direction that increasingly ignores the soul, the spiritual dimension of people, and views a person as nothing more than a body whose expressions of vitality come forth from matter. In this way the entirely sacred character is eliminated from suffering. All preparation for dying becomes unimaginable. Suicide is proclaimed to be innocent in principle. Sensuousness is loosened from every restraint, as though justified by the demand of well-being. And all prayer by and for the sick is denigrated as child's play.

Even though this evil is less prevalent among the discipline of natural science, because it suffices the most with observation and experimentation, nevertheless we must not forget that the discipline of natural science is becoming increasingly occupied with the fundamental problems of life. Its theory of evolution, as though all human life should have arisen automatically from cells and atoms apart from any higher ordination, leads directly to atheism, destroys the creation made by God's almighty power, and denies that we were formed according to the image of God, and along with that, the highest value of our being human. By means of this foundational theory, natural science dominates every other discipline now, and aligns itself in principle polemically against every Christian confession.

As far as the discipline of the humanities is concerned, we need mention only three elements—language, history, and philosophy—in order to make immediately plain the danger it yields as soon as it leaves the path of the truth. The teaching about the origin of human language, as provided by the practitioners of this discipline in various forms, corresponds almost reflexively to the evolutionary theory of the natural science practitioners, portraying the human person as originally making sounds half resembling animals, reaching something close to human language only after a centuries-long development.

In the treatment of history, every notion that the history of the human race is arranged around the cross of Golgotha as its midpoint, designed this way by God's ordination that ought to be respected, is gradually being destroyed. In its place we get a perspective of history that explains the entire course of things on the basis of purely material and psychological causes. When it comes to philosophy, it hardly needs to be recalled how this discipline, as it increasingly sets aside all revelation, has repeatedly spun from its own theoretical axiom assumptions concerning the entirety of reality. Despite the incidental benefit of these assumptions, in its fundamental concept and scope philosophy has established itself in opposition against our Christian confession.

With regard to the damaging influence that the imbalanced extolling of the classical idolatrous world of Greece has had on our youth, we say not a word in this context. After all, here the evil lies not in this classical study itself, but in the wrong use non-Christian perspectives have made of such study.

All of this is simply the further outworking of what we posited above as the general rule, namely, that unbelieving science and the science done by believing Christians are two, and cannot flow alongside each other within one river bed. Even the suggested notion that this evil could be countered by placing a few Christian thinkers to function as a corrective within the schools of unbelieving science rests upon self-deception. Naturally it is readily admitted that something like this is better than nothing. This can serve as a temporary means of assistance and by this means evil can be minimized, at least in terms of the training of students. Young people nurtured in Christian homes who, left to themselves, would quickly drown in the waters of unbelieving academic life, could obtain support from such assistant instructors for their resistance, and be armed by them against the temptation to which they are exposed. But science itself is not guided in this way, and thus continues to operate on a false basis.

Add to this the general impression that science proper comes forth from the unbelieving world, as though the power and impulse for science come from the unbelieving world, as though unbelieving science builds the temple of science, and as though in this respect the Christian religion had no other and no higher calling than to offer criticism here and there, and if possible, to introduce modest correction. The tree remains evil, and continues to thrive from its mistaken root, and the only thing we get to do is to pinch off a few shoots, prune a few nettles, and here and there fasten to its branches some flowers we have plucked from elsewhere, which, if you are honest, are naturally destined to wither again. No, what we need is an edifice of the whole of science built on a Christian foundation. We need the plant of science to be flourishing from its Christian root. For us to be satisfied with the role of strolling through someone else's garden with pruning shears in hand is simply to discard the honor and the value of our Christian religion.

WHAT WE NEED IS AN EDIFICE OF THE WHOLE OF SCIENCE BUILT ON A CHRISTIAN FOUNDATION. WE NEED THE PLANT OF SCIENCE TO BE FLOURISHING FROM ITS CHRISTIAN ROOT.

If for every lectern occupied by an unbelieving educator we could set up our own lectern for a believing educator, then the matter would be very different. For at that point we would have a full complement of disciplines, and what would prevent those departments from joining together as their own university, even if you would have to do this for an entirely different reason? As long as you permit the unbelieving university to be the sole university, and station your people there as a corrective, the lectures given by the unbelieving educators continue to be the required lessons, and those lectures given by your people remain merely elective. The former bear the stamp of what is proper and essential, since they provide the core material, while the latter are merely added as a supplement.

If you deliver no more than a few lectures, that would be fine but not very profitable, as we have shown. But if you occupy all of the counter-lecterns, then it would naturally result in a parallel set of lessons that simply could not all be taken by the students, for which there would not be enough hours. Above all, do not forget that by placing a few isolated instructors of your own over against the teaching of others you would not change the status of final exams. Not your people, but the officially appointed instructors would continue to administer those exams.

Anyone familiar with the life of public universities knows full well how the examinations dominate all the course work here, and how studying for these exams lays claim to virtually the whole time of students. Given this reality, how would you ever create the possibility for the lectures of your people to be effectively corrective rather than being anything more than superficial and avocational?

This is why a better future and a stronger position can be obtained by believing Christianity only when Christianity is permeated by its calling to bring the power of its faith to independent expression also in the arena of science. To keep thinking that by functioning in a purely critical way we will ultimately convince unbelieving educators of their error is nothing but pure illusion. They are unable to perceive the truth regarding the basis of everything, and therefore they cannot be convinced by us. With a kind of color blindness they oppose our sacred things, and they are being entirely upright when they confess not to see what you see, and therefore to judge that you are mistaken about what you think you see. Reconciliation that would lead to agreement is completely inconceivable at this point. We are facing a gaping crevasse that cannot be bridged. As long as Christianity refuses to accept this duality with full conviction with all its consequences, it will be repeatedly punished with the invasion of her own territory by unbelieving science, with the falsification of its theology, with the undermining of its confession, and with the weakening of its faith.

So we must view it, then, as a fortunate consequence of the operation of common grace that unbelieving science increasingly shakes off every remnant of the Christian tradition, breaking more and more publicly with the categories that have been handed down. With escalating determination, unbelieving science substitutes a completely atheistic worldview for ours, and makes our continued lodging in her tents increasingly impossible. This, after all, is how it will increasingly press Christians to take a stand within their own territory. And what Christianity would never have done on its own impulse it will finally accomplish under the pressure of an increasingly bold unbelief that denies all that is sacred. All of this means that Christians will begin to perceive the inexorable need to begin pursuing science independently on the basis of their own principles, leading them to strive for a university life that honors the mystery of all wisdom and all science in Christ.

PART TWO
ART

six

WONDER

For how great is his goodness,
and how great his beauty!
Zechariah 9:17a

ᘉ

THE TOPIC OF ART also requires special attention in connection with common grace.

We chose art not because we attached less importance to the topics of *religion* and *moral living,* nor because we denied that a measure of religion and of moral living is conceivable under the blessing of common grace—even absent higher light. This is continually apparent with regard to individuals, whole groups, and even nations. Those regions of Africa where Islam has penetrated, for example, may lag far behind, compared to Christian Europe, but it cannot be disputed that they demonstrate a much higher religious and moral character than the dark-skinned tribes of Central Africa.* And here in Europe, among families that have made a complete break with the confession of Christ, you occasionally meet men and women whose religious life is highly developed and whose moral standpoint often commands respect. Nevertheless, we did not devote a separate study here either to religion or to the moral life because the phenomena that would be discussed have already been covered fully in doctrinal works. Therefore, a separate discussion here would be merely a summary or a repetition, which we wish to avoid.†

---

*Here Kuyper is invoking the idea, popularized at the turn of the twentieth century, that monotheistic religions, including Islam, were more developed and superior forms of religion than indigenous and polytheistic religions.

†Kuyper is referring to sections of his larger three-volume work on common grace. For more on the translation of this work, see "About the Common Grace Translation Project," p. 183.

Art, however, is an entirely different matter. This topic was touched upon here and there only incidentally, but it requires a separate discussion. This discussion is needed all the more because the appreciation of *art* in the religious realm varies widely. Particularly in Reformed church circles this seems to have resulted in the condemnation, if not banishment, of art.

Religion and art are so closely related that art still gratefully acknowledges how it owes its origins to public worship. It is therefore no secret how religion and art were intertwined within the pagan world at virtually every point. Scripture tells us how in Israel art was concentrated exclusively in the temple on Mount Zion. Beyond the ministry of the sacred, art lay virtually fallow. And even now the Greek Orthodox Church, the Roman Catholic Church, and to some extent also the Lutheran churches show what an exalted significance art holds for the development of the religious sentiments.

Within Islam art lost much of its significance in the sacred realm due to the strong opposition against any use of images and representations. But even among Reformed Christians, in spite of the fact that their form of worship had a strictly spiritual character, the arts of architecture, singing, and music have been incorporated on a relatively large scale in public worship. It is well-known how much value John Calvin attached to singing in church, how much effort he exerted to elevate singing to a higher art form, and how especially Goudimel supported him in this effort.*

Nevertheless Von Hartmann's comment is correct that in its highest form, religion lays aside the robe of art and ends up occu-

---

*Claude Goudimel (ca. 1514-1572) was a French composer, editor, and publisher who is most famous for his four-part setting of the Genevan Psalter.

pying an entirely independent position vis-à-vis art.* Indeed, this cannot be otherwise. By virtue of the ordinance of creation, the religious awareness created within us matures by *two* means. A knowledge of God speaks to us from the nature of created things, for "his invisible attributes, namely, his eternal power and divine nature, have been clearly perceived, ever since the creation of the world, in the things that have been made" (Rom. 1:20). This is the first means.

And alongside it stood in paradise, as a second means, the spiritual revelation in and to the heart of people. The consequences of sin, however, were that eyes and ears became closed to this revelation, and other than a tradition of this spiritual revelation, nothing remained except the revelation of God in nature. But this in turn also became darkened, partly because the capacity to know God through nature diminished, partly because the curse came upon the earth and drew a veil over its beauty. Had common grace not intervened to inwardly strengthen religious consciousness and to outwardly safeguard the speech of nature from falling silent, all religion would have disappeared in short order.

But now, thanks to the operation of common grace, virtually all peoples display a certain need for religion, religion that in its weakened and mutilated form is in almost all respects linked to divine revelation through *nature*. Sun, moon, and stars beckon people to worship the Creator—until people lose sight of the living God and begin to worship the sun, moon, and stars themselves. Even in Israel not a few worshiped the moon as the Queen

---

*Karl Robert Eduard von Hartmann (1842-1906) was a German philosopher who was most well-known for his concept of the Unconscious. He had considerable influence upon Carl Jung (1875-1961), the Swiss psychiatrist and originator of analytical psychology.

of Heaven* (Jer. 7:18, 44:15-18). The bull as type of the procreative force of nature was soon worshiped under the name Apis, and what was called calf worship in Israel was nothing but an imitation of this pagan form of worship.

Especially in the East, where the beauty, richness, and lushness of nature make an impression that is so much more powerful than in our northern and western countries, this worship of nature emerged spontaneously. And even in the far North, where ice is the greatest natural phenomenon, glaciers and icebergs gave birth to a religious imagery that ultimately was nothing but nature worship. The veneration and worship of the human being, toward which humanity advanced especially in Greece, but known, albeit in modified form, in India as well, stood on a higher plane than the *animal* worship in the East. This despite the indisputable contradiction that humanity's self-elevation was coupled with, and at the same time was counteracting, the element that is so important in religion, namely, consciousness of human dependency.

Nevertheless, in whatever form idolatrous religion appeared, precisely because it was derived from the external, and increasingly lost the factor of spiritual revelation, it could develop in no other way than in *visible* forms. It continued to require a visible object of worship, which led to image worship in various forms. Without an image of their idol, people were ultimately unable to imagine their idol. The worshiping multitude possessed nothing more in itself. Everything had to be performed before their eyes. So all religion came increasingly to be concentrated in a sacred place, in a consecrated building, in consecrated persons, in sacred images and altars, and in the sacred performances occurring at those altars. This explains the deep significance ascribed to the temple, and to idol images and altars, to various instruments of

---

*Hebrew: *Malkath haShamayim*

worship, to the priestly garments, to their music, to their song, to their performances. There was scarcely any spiritual adoration any longer. Everything had to be seen and heard, viewed and admired in ecstasy.

To the extent that the multitude was kept amazed by those hallowed phenomena and kept its money flowing for this worship, to that extent competition arose between cities and among temples. This led in turn for the first time to making a huge sum of money available in connection with this consecrated domain, money needed by art for rendering its impressive performances. It is no surprise, then, that architecture, sculpture, painting, music, and poetry flourished initially within temple worship, developing into more refined forms in which it sought to realize its ideal. A religion fed in its idolatrous form only exclusively by nature or by human megalomania can seek its glory nowhere else than in external pageantry. This explains why the marriage between art and religion in its essential nature belongs to every kind of idolatry.

———————

Let us not confuse the temple ministry on Mount Zion with this. Due to the absence of any visible object of worship, the worship on Mount Zion pointed precisely to the invisible and spiritual. The form and ministry that was developed on Zion, all the way to its smallest detail, never bore anything other than a *symbolic* character.

The word *symbol* means the coinciding of two distinct spheres of life. A symbol declares to you, first, that besides this visible world there exists an invisible, spiritual world as well; second, that between this visible and invisible world a particular connection exists; and third, that visible

A SYMBOL IS ALWAYS SOMETHING VISIBLE THAT FUNCTIONS AS A SIGN, IMAGE, OR DENOTATION OF SOMETHING SPIRITUAL AND INVISIBLE.

signs can portray spiritual things for us. So a symbol is always something visible that functions as a sign, image, or denotation of something spiritual and invisible.

Whereas idol worship leads away from the spiritual, obscures the spiritual, and drives it into the background, symbolic worship by contrast possesses the capacity, by repeatedly connecting the visible symbol with the spiritual, to direct a people still dependent on the sensuous toward the spiritual and to nurture that people unto the spiritual.

Understood this way, the worship that occurred in the temple on Zion was to that extent definitely and precisely spiritual in its orientation. God dwelt there, and yet no one saw God, not even the high priest when he entered the Holy of Holies. It was exactly this worship of the Unseen and the Unseeable that imparted to this worship its spiritual character. In our Christian religion, the water of baptism and the bread and wine of the Eucharist are such visible symbols, representing to us the washing away of our sins and the suffering and dying of Christ for our sins. Nevertheless the relationship between the symbol and the spiritual reality now is different.

For us, spiritual adoration stands in the foreground, whereas for Israel everything spiritual was still presented before the eyes of the people in shadows and in symbols. In those shadows and symbols the image of the coming Messiah was expressed. After he had come, the curtain of the temple was torn, and the temple on Zion was destroyed in order never again to be rebuilt. Anyone who after Christ's coming still continued to depend on the symbol and shadow of the Messiah demonstrated that he did not understand his coming, thereby denying and rejecting him.

This explains the sacred struggle waged by Paul against this nonsense especially among the churches of Galatia. Continuing to hold on to the symbolic showed a spiritual disposition incompatible with faith in the Lamb of God. By contrast, until the coming of Christ, art possessed its high calling to express the symbolism of Zion's temple in a beautiful manner, and the art of Egypt together with the art of Hiram from Tyre, was made subservient to what was honored on Mount Zion as "the perfection of beauty" in Solomon's temple and earlier already in the tabernacle.*

From this it also followed that once fulfillment had arrived, the symbolic element receded, and worship in spirit and truth rose above the production of art and achieved its current independence. Alongside the knowledge of God from nature, the knowledge of God was available in spiritual revelation, and when that spiritual revelation reached its pinnacle and perfection in Christ, religion had to turn inward so that in worship the expression of spiritual life had to stand in the foreground. To the extent that this spiritual expression still required a form, such form also had to be beautiful, which in turn led to calling upon the assistance of art, albeit in an entirely *serving* capacity. It was not expected that art would manifest and reveal the divine. Any kind of domination by art had to be denied. Henceforth, performing a helping service was art's sole calling.

Nevertheless, even after Christ came, religion could not yet climb to that free, independent position at once. In the eastern Mediterranean region, where the Christian church obtained its first expansion, as well as in southern Europe and in Asia Minor, along with the northern coast of Africa, the multitudes were far too accustomed to the visual portrayal of the sacred, and were too dependent on visual and artistic forms as well. As a result, the vanquished temple pageantry soon resurfaced amid the opulence of the churches. Decorative forms and garments were esteemed

---

*See 1 Kings 7:13-47.

highly. Numerous symbols, and eventually painting and sculpture, soon made their entrance once again.

To be sure, a vigorous reaction arose at that point, one that led to a terrible struggle between the spiritual and the sensuous in the well-known iconoclastic controversy. But the purely spiritual had to suffer defeat in the opulent eastern Mediterranean region, such that the worship of the Greek Orthodox Church and the Roman Catholic Church is largely shaped by the outcome of that struggle. This was not because people in either the Greek or the Roman church had ever given all those external phenomena any theoretical explanation other than a symbolic significance. But practically such an ornate symbolism always confronts a fundamentally spiritual religion with the danger that the spiritual will once again be overtaken by the sensuous. Anyone, especially in southern countries, who carefully observed the use of this symbolism sensed immediately how once this symbolism takes over it leads people back into idolatry again.

The spiritual reaction to this danger was one of the motives of the Reformation. This spiritual reaction had been prepared already by the mysticism of the Middle Ages. But only when this mysticism was strengthened by the concentrated drive of the heart in pursuit of God did this reaction exert power sufficient for the spiritual to break through the barrier of the sensuous. It was that spiritual reaction, then, that took up the struggle rather suddenly against such sensuous worship, gathering up the wares, as Jeremiah 10:17 puts it, especially among Reformed churches, more so than among Lutheran churches.

Related to this was the reality that the Reformation made hardly any headway in southern Europe, and was established almost exclusively in northern Europe where the need for portraying the sensuous was less developed in the people's natural disposition. Since that time, this domination of the spiritual element has been again repulsed, but for the rest one could say that it has continued in Scandinavia, in northern Germany, in our country, in Scotland, and in America. One could add also that the more developed the Christian religion became, the more it was freed from the need for the sensuous form, and the more it sought and seeks its ideal in terms of spiritual beauty.

Consequently we observe in this course of events a process that obeys a natural law. As long as the religious idea draws its strength only from beholding nature, religion performed in the idolatrous temples bears a merely sensuous character and art dominates within the temple.

As soon as spiritual revelation returned in Israel, a spiritual sphere came to stand alongside the sphere of the sensuous, and both spheres found their interconnected expression in the rich symbolism of Zion's temple. As the spiritual revelation reached its culmination in Christ, the symbolic was pushed back by the spiritual, and the apostolic epistles show us nothing less than a purely spiritual veneration among the apostolic churches. As soon, however, as the church expanded among the nations, who were already by nature dependent on the sensuous, lush symbolism crept back into the church. During the iconoclastic controversy, the spiritual reaction appeared powerless to cast off the yoke, so that worship continued to display a highly symbolic character for many centuries.

However, after the Reformation a new spiritual reaction arose that this time triumphed, introducing in northern Europe a kind of worship that sought its power only in the spiritual beauty of the soul. Once it had achieved this position, spiritual veneration was increasingly able to survive, leading with observable progress increasingly to despising all outward display and to establishing worship in spirit and in truth to be the core of worship.

This process leads to the question: does this course of events warrant the conclusion that therefore art is condemned, and art is to be considered by spiritually oriented Christians as an evil to be opposed?

> DOES THIS COURSE OF EVENTS WARRANT THE CONCLUSION THAT THEREFORE ART IS CONDEMNED, AND ART IS TO BE CONSIDERED BY SPIRITUALLY ORIENTED CHRISTIANS AS AN EVIL TO BE OPPOSED?

That question can be answered only in the affirmative if one views art merely as a parasite that can grow only by being attached to the stem of ecclesiastical life. Burdening the sacred with what drives the spiritual into the background, all for the sake of the growth of art, is the honorable reputation of religion, in which case we must declare without hesitation that it would be better for all art to disappear than that the spiritual character of our Christian religion would be injured. A people can live and grow without art, if necessary, but not without religion.

But is that the proper question? Or should we not rather acknowledge that in its initial appearance, art was powerless in learning to walk had it not been held by the reins of the priest? Should we not acknowledge that once it had achieved further development, art could appeal in every possible way to an independent, free, and autonomous existence?

To see this clearly, we obviously need to investigate the essence of art more deeply, something we can undertake only in a subsequent section. But at this point we can already observe that so much of art with its diversity could emerge at first like an ivy vine curling around the sacred, and only in a later stage of development grow into an entirely independent plant.

In this connection we recall education with all its branches, an enterprise that initially among both pagans and Christians leaned upon and was supported by the sacred and the holy, but thereafter came to stand on its own legs, and only in that independent position developed its proper essence. Only because art was itself religion, and thus constituted an integral element of religion, could its right of independence be contested. By contrast, everyone knows how rarely one finds pious and zealous confessors of the Lord's name in the art world, and conversely, how in broad circles of the artist's life even the moral ordinances are treated lightly. From this we can already surmise how by nature the artistic genius and the spirit of divine adoption are scarcely twin sisters.

So the outcome has shown how, after receiving their divorce papers from the ecclesiastical domain at the time of the Reformation, the arts hardly disappeared from view. Far rather was it the case that art everywhere ensured that henceforth it could lead an independent existence. The outcome has shown the wonderful ways that art has succeeded in this endeavor.

It cannot be entirely denied that this has led in part to making art a worldly pursuit, indeed, to secularizing art, to say nothing of misusing art to satisfy sinful desires. We will return to this as well.

But let it be said that in no case can this abuse of freedom be advanced as proof that art has no right to its independent existence. In our human life there is nothing, absolutely nothing, that eventually does not misuse for sinful purposes the freedom it acquires. Observe how time and again freedom of conscience is abused for blasphemy, or, if you will, how the sovereignty that God grants to a prince or a ruler is abused for oppressing, tyrannizing, and weakening a people. By itself it is completely true that after its liberation, art became worldly, in this sense, that it ceased to inhabit sacred space and came to be mixed in with ordinary civic life.

The inspiration of art never belonged to particular grace, but always proceeded from common grace. It is exactly everyday human living that constitutes the broad arena where common grace shines, and simultaneously the arena where art constructs its own temple as well.

This in no way entails, however, that therefore art henceforth should be permitted to derive its motives no longer from the sacred, or that art no longer possesses a calling to glorify God's name. Leaving aside architecture for the moment, which naturally comes up in connection with building churches, there is not only art of a higher order that, from the moment it began to reveal its independent character, has at the same time received its richest motives from the holy and the sacred. It could not have been otherwise.

Artistic genius and nobility of soul are not mutually exclusive, and wherever artistic genius may dwell within a noble soul, how could the artistic eye be closed to the entirely singular exaltedness that focuses on the name of Christ? Why should an image, an embroidered scene, an oratorio, or a hymn be produced only for ecclesiastical use in order to inspire the gifted creator of these artifacts with sacred passion? Art also enjoys its lower and higher spheres of development, and how could it be any other way than that in its higher spheres art *must* ascend to the sublime, and in that sublimity it automatically encounters the wonders of religion, incorporates them, and reproduces them in artistic form?

The separation between church and art, therefore, does not at all bear the character of a complete separation between art and religion. Instead, the bond between both is guaranteed in the ideal character of both, so that if people refuse to permit the refined religious impulse to affect art, that defect belongs not to art as such but to the impiety of those advocates.

Only this much we admit, namely, that in its beginning stages, the course of the Reformation did cause disorder and confusion. The generation of that time, because it was accustomed to finding art mainly in the church building, and because it was driven to opposition out of spiritual aversion toward this art in the churches, risked the very serious peril after the churches were purified of condemning art as such. This peril was partially realized. At that time there was a certain aversion toward art that had arisen from a religious motive, a hostility that still continues to function in some circles even today. On the other hand, even less can it be denied that the art that had been newly set free entered all too quickly into the service of licentiousness and discarded its honor.

This should not surprise us. Anyone who at long last emerges from a guardianship that lasted far too long and was far too strict is easily inclined toward debauchery, and often the proper use of the new-found freedom lies beyond reach. How often did not our academicians behave in those early years like young boys who up until then had been kept inside the house too long, but suddenly found themselves in an academic setting, released from every form of discipline, to be their own lord and master? What shameful scenes have people not witnessed of soldiers who, after victory, were released by their commanders from the constraints of discipline?

Therefore this argument fails to deliver any irrefutable proof at all against the claim that, even though for centuries art was unable to survive in our churches apart from the support of the temple ministry and later of the activities of worship, nevertheless art has been summoned to freedom. This claim is coupled with the insistence that in this way the separation between religion and art brought about by the Reformation was the inevitable effect of a natural process in a twofold sense. First, religion could confess its spiritual character only to the degree it was separated. And second, art could attain its rightful independence only to the degree it was separated.

So, then, especially in the sixteenth century, art moved out of the tent of the sacred to erect its own tent in the domain of common grace, where it belongs. This was a phenomenon whose simultaneous consequence was that only when art was flourishing in the domain of common grace did it yearn for its significance to extend to all of human living in broader society. For what people term the democratizing of art became a fact for the first time in the nineteenth century, even though the expansion of art's territory began already in the sixteenth century. Our Dutch school of painters from those days prove that claim, both in terms of the diversity of motives whereby these artists were inspired and in terms of the broader circle of citizens who adorned their rooms with the objects of art.

> SO, THEN, ESPECIALLY IN THE SIXTEENTH CENTURY, ART MOVED OUT OF THE TENT OF THE SACRED TO ERECT ITS OWN TENT IN THE DOMAIN OF COMMON GRACE, WHERE IT BELONGS..

seven

BEAUTY

For the creation was subjected to futility, not willingly, but because of him who subjected it, in hope that the creation itself will be set free from its bondage to corruption and obtain the freedom of the glory of the children of God.

Romans 8:20-21

CR

IF THEREFORE WE MUST ACCORD to art an independent existence, and along with it grant the arena of beauty an independent character, then we need to investigate what view of beauty, and consequently, what view of art itself, we should construct.

In broader society people tend to employ the contrast between *flesh* and *spirit*, assigning beauty to the desires of the flesh, resulting in far less appreciation of beauty and greater inclination to condemn it. The fact that despite this way of thinking, people repeatedly feel attracted by beauty does not contradict this assessment. For people acknowledge that the sinful heart is susceptible to every form of lust, but confess afterward to having fallen. "Flesh and spirit," when viewed as being in absolute contradiction, involve a judgment regarding everything that charms eye or ear. The spirit is then viewed as the only good, the flesh as the fountain of all evil. Beauty makes this fountain of evil even more alluring, becoming the siren that through its lovely sound seeks to lure us into the depths unto destruction.

In terms of this position, the spirit comes from God, the flesh from the devil. Your piety rises in value to the degree that you increasingly become spirit and get rid of everything that is fleshly. Your body is therefore a prison that cages the soul, and that soul flees toward the moment when death will deliver it from prison. That body must be nourished as little as possible, and its garments must consist simply of covering without beauty in form or color, especially without adornment. For the sake of preserving the sacred within us, the ugly is preferable to the beautiful. Ugliness is the good angel who keeps us near God, beauty is the wicked angel who leads us away from God. Despite the fascination that the wicked angel may hold for us, everyone senses that only the good angels deserve our sympathy.

The question, however, is this: is such a view correct? Simply to ridicule anyone who holds this view provides no judgment of any moral significance. And when people in our modern time who idolize art and are therefore ready, for the sake of the ideal of beauty, to forget the Father of spirits, even though in Christian circles they may be inclined to sing along in that choir giving echo to the praise of art, this says nothing to the man or woman with a serious view of life.

We still continue to confront the fact that in circles of art aficionados, the first commandment, that we love God with all our heart, soul, and strength, is followed much more loosely than in circles where people are blind and deaf toward the world of beauty. Even among Christians one observes not infrequently the phenomenon that a gleam rises in the eye and a warmth comes to the voice when objects of art or of beauty are discussed, whereas that same eye so often goes dim and that tone turns cold when discussion shifts to the sacred things of God.

Plainly, practical experience would be unable to do anything else than maintain a position against art for the sake of the truth. This would lead our perspective about art to a different conclusion, depending on whether we were to argue neither on the basis of complacency toward the tone that dominates at present, nor on the basis of culpable concession toward the world's view, but exclusively out of obedience to God's Word. We are not in the least joining the side of those who are in fact idolizing art, but rather we decisively join the side of those who put the honor of God above all else. It is exclusively the firm conviction that beauty comes from God and not from the Devil that forbids us to apply the contrast between "flesh and spirit" in its absolute sense here.

It is true that Scripture repeatedly warns us not to be carried away by the sensuous world. In contrast to the man with a gold ring on his finger, the poor man who looks in vain for a place in God's house finds provision. In Jesus' estimation, the poor man Lazarus, with his rags and sores, stands far above the rich man who is enjoying his resplendent meal clothed in the finest of garments. Women are warned to seek their adornment not in the braiding of their hair and in golden jewelry, but in a quiet spirit that is precious before God. We are told that the world with all its desires is passing away, and conversely, that whoever does the will of God abides forever. This contrast is pressed further by declaring that "all that is in the world—the desires of the flesh and the desires of the eyes and pride in possessions—is not from the Father but is from the world" (1 John 2:16). Consequently, never can accommodation to worldly sensuousness be justified or even excused among those who confess the Lord.

This does not decide the matter in principle, however. All of this refers to a *misuse* that is disapproved and warned against, but all of this is definitely opposed to *lawful use*.

One can sense this immediately if we contrast Jesus with John the Baptizer. John the Baptizer was an ascetic. He lived in the desert, was clothed with

JESUS SAT DOWN AT FEASTS, ATTENDED A WEDDING, ATE FINE FOODS, DRANK WINE, AND USED MONEY THAT FRIENDS GAVE HIM. HIS DEMEANOR WAS SO FASHIONABLE THAT THE CLOTHES STRIPPED FROM HIM BEFORE HE WAS HUNG ON THE CROSS WERE THOUGHT DESIRABLE ENOUGH TO DIVIDE AMONG THE SOLDIERS WHO PERFORMED THE EXECUTION ON GOLGOTHA.

animal skins, ate grasshoppers and honey, and withdrew from ordinary activities of the world. By contrast, Jesus sat down at feasts, attended a wedding, ate fine foods, drank wine, and used money that friends gave him. His demeanor was so fashionable that the clothes stripped from him before he was hung on the cross were thought desirable enough to divide among the soldiers who performed the execution on Golgotha.

The world-denying asceticism of John is not thereby condemned. This too had its value and significance at that moment. But it is nevertheless clear that Jesus did not make this asceticism the standard for living. People even accused Jesus of being a glutton and a drunkard.

The solution to the issue confronting us must therefore be sought elsewhere.

Let us note in the first place, then, that Scripture ascribes to the Devil no creative capacity. The world of beauty that does in fact exist can have originated nowhere else than in the creation of God. The world of beauty was thus conceived by God, determined by his decree, called into being by him, and is maintained by him.

Beauty definitely does not exist only in what human inspiration or human ability produces, but also exists in the natural world that is a direct creation of God himself. The splendor of the firmament and the sparkling world of the starry sky are his. Jesus himself drew our attention to the beauty radiating in the plant world, when he spoke of the lilies of the field that neither toil nor spin, that nevertheless surpass the beauty of Solomon's splendorous array. The beauty of nature is occasionally so overwhelming that the thirsty spirit cannot escape the sense of amazement. The heavens declare God's glory, and the firmament his handiwork.*

---

*See Matthew 6:28-29 and Psalm 19:1.

Not only the general appearance of nature, whether in its summer garb or its winter apparel, can be so delightfully beautiful, but the individual parts of the organisms that God created are so exquisite in their beauty as well.

One need only consider the plumage of so many birds, the fur of so many animals, the eye of the deer, or the lion's mane. Add to this man himself, who observes and appreciates all kinds of beauty, who is a product of this beautiful creation. Scripture continually comments about the beauty of women, mentioning that Sara was "very beautiful," that Absalom had a "beautiful sister," that "such beautiful women" as Job's second set of daughters were not found in all the land of Uz. The handsome beauty of men like Absalom is renowned in Scripture, and the little child Moses is said to have attracted Pharaoh's daughter by his beauty and loveliness. Therefore, not only is beauty observed as part of human appearance, but that beauty is also highlighted in Scripture as something attractive. From this it follows that beauty was designed by God to be something powerful, having arisen from the pleasure of God, having been intentionally willed by God and having been called into existence by his almighty power.

This already forbids us to condemn beauty as such, since beauty is a creation of God. We cannot even say that God created this beauty merely for our amusement. God himself must enjoy beauty. Did not beauty shimmer and glisten century after century on mountain tops and in remote places never trod by human feet? Neither the North Pole nor the South Pole have yet been seen by human beings, so who can describe the splendor and majesty in that unexplored glacial world that has shimmered before God's eye already for centuries past and for centuries to come? What do we really know about the stars in the Milky Way, or even about the planets that are together with us orbiting around the sun?

Despite such ignorance on our part, what dizzying beauty adorns that starry universe!

———

That is how it is with beauty. And it is no different with our *sense* of beauty. It is an undeniable fact that a notion and a sense of beauty are unique to us as human beings. That notion and that sense do not function equally strongly among everybody. They seem to be entirely jaded among a few. Nevertheless, the yearning to adorn our homes or our clothes, or to make ourselves "beautiful" with gold, silver, or precious jewels, is common to all peoples. That can be observed even among the most primitive tribes.

Everyone listens to the song of the lark, the blackbird, or the nightingale. Among all peoples the beautiful young woman has been the epitome of attractiveness. No matter how superficial the taste of many may be, a certain appreciation for beauty is still a shared feature of our human nature. We observe this sense of beauty develop. Among civilized peoples beauty grows in power and expands in scope. In a few circles that sense of beauty has gradually reached the form of artistic appreciation. The Greeks have always been the people among the nations who seemed to possess the most classical sense of beauty. At the top of this pyramid stand ultimately the inspired art connoisseurs who are moved by the fine tuning and softest shimmering of beauty.

From where does that sense of beauty come? Can something belonging to our human nature be anything else than an *innate* capacity? If it has been created in us, by whom else was it deposited within us than by the One who created us? Now if, on the one hand, we find within God himself the ordinance governing beauty, so that he has stamped it upon his creation like a divine imprint, and if, on the other hand, we find in every human being a sense of beauty that has been created in us by God, what else could that concept of beauty within us be than one of the features of God's image according to which we have been created?

At this point we must take note of something else entirely different. The world we inhabit is not the only world that Scripture teaches us about. Rather, Scripture directs our attention away from this world, which is passing, to a new world that is coming. All that now exists will perish in a cosmic fire. "The heavens will be set on fire and dissolved, and the heavenly bodies will melt as they burn!" (2 Pet. 3:12). Then from this cosmic fire will appear "according to his promise . . . new heavens and a new earth in which righteousness dwells" (2 Pet. 3:13).

What image is used to portray for us that new earth? Surely not one that is simply spiritual. No, rather an earth that thoroughly resembles a visible, external, observable creation. Who can fathom the portrait given us in John's Apocalypse of the New Jerusalem with its foundations of emerald and sapphire and its pearly gates, without being immediately overwhelmed with the impression of a glorious beauty that will far surpass the most beautiful thing our eyes have ever seen?

Scripture even uses a special word for that more exalted beauty of the coming world, and repeatedly describes what will come at that time as *the kingdom of glory*. No matter how beautiful in many respects this earth may already be, it is not yet glorious. That more exalted beauty, called "glory," comes only in the hereafter. To such an extent even that those who belong to Christ will arise at that time and will dwell in a regenerated body that will be conformed to the glorified body of Christ. In the Revelation of John we receive a picture of that glorified body of Christ, one that is so astounding and overwhelming in its appearance that when John beheld it, he fell to the ground as though dead.

The tenor of Holy Scripture, therefore, hardly suggests that beauty is something that passes away, something we leave behind at our death, never to find it again. On the contrary, according to the tenor of Scripture, beauty belongs to the eternal things, things that perish here in order later to return eternally in a more exalted form, and only then to make the full glorifying of God's majesty radiate throughout his creation.

According to Scripture, then, beauty cannot be separated from God. "Out of Zion, the perfection of beauty, God shines forth" (Ps. 50:2). "For how great," Zechariah cries out, "is his goodness, and how great his beauty!" (Zech. 9:17). Of the Messiah it is said, "You are the most handsome of the sons of men" (Ps. 45:2). "Splendor and majesty," says the Psalmist, "are before him" (Ps. 96:6). "His glory [is] above the heavens" (Ps. 113:4). Even in the Lord's Prayer, Jesus teaches us to pray that not only the kingdom and the power, but also the glory of God may endure forever!

Glory is, in fact, nothing other than a higher degree of beauty. It is beauty in its consummation, but still in a way whereby *present* beauty and *coming* glory are connected to one another, such that both are revelations of one and the same principle. This found clear expression on Mount Tabor. There Christ appeared suddenly in glory, and yet a moment later that glory was again extinguished, and Jesus stood once again before the eyes of his disciples in his resplendent earthly form. So we see earthly beauty ascending to glory, and a moment later that glorious form descend again to the resplendent earthly form.*

By means of his resurrection, Jesus arose in the same body that had hung on the cross, and he appeared in glory to John on Patmos with this continually identical body. This makes us think of an uncut diamond that is soon to be cut. Remaining the very same stone, the finely cut diamond radiates an entirely different glory.

---

*See Matthew 17:1-9.

People realize in advance that a diamond is nothing but a piece of coal, which is transformed into carbon through intense heat and exposure to oxygen in the air. If a piece of coal can become a diamond simply through the application of elemental natural forces, and by some polishing that diamond can obtain a most elegant luster, what would prevent God from transforming what is now on earth into the exalted luster of his glory? When Scripture tells us that the precious jewels that are now so rare on earth will be the ordinary building material in the New Jerusalem, we receive the very same mental picture that the minerals will remain the same, and that through a new chemical process, from what now exists the exalted heavenly divine glory will sparkle.

So it is remarkable that when Paul speaks of the knowledge of God that we obtain from nature, he refers not only to the "eternal power," but also to the divine deity that is stamped on all of creation like an imprint. Beauty, and beyond that, divine glory is the Spirit radiating through what appears before our eyes.

In this connection, however, we must also take into account the rupture that has occurred in the original creation. The earth as it now appears to us is no longer what paradise was. Regarding the original paradise situation no accurate data has been transmitted to us, except that Scripture tells us clearly that the word "paradise" referred to a more beautiful state of affairs than we now encounter. When in the Song of Songs the Bridegroom speaks of "an orchard [*paradise*] of pomegranates, with all choicest fruits, henna with nard" (Song of Sol. 4:13), apparently he intends a poetic elevation of the real situation. When the criminal hanging alongside Jesus on the cross speaks of paradise (Luke 23:43), he was referring to the situation of the blessed. When Paul testifies that he was taken up into paradise by the rapture of all his senses (2 Cor. 12:3), that expression indicates a state of heavenly glory. Finally, when Jesus instructs John on Patmos to write to the church in Ephesus that to the one who conquers it will be given to eat of the tree of life that is in the middle of the paradise of God (Rev. 2:7), that word indicates a world that far surpasses this world in glory.

From all of this we may surmise that the world as God created it was far more beautiful than the world in which we now dwell. With this the paradise story corresponds insofar as we read there how after their fall into sin, Adam and Eve were driven out of paradise and thereafter had to inhabit an earth that was burdened with the curse. We should understand this curse to entail a diminishing of harmony and thereby a diminishing of beauty.

Nevertheless, we may not deduce from this that paradise was then what the kingdom of glory will be. Perhaps one could make that deduction on the basis of the fact that twice Jesus used the term *paradise* to refer to that coming glory, but such an inference is mistaken.

We can see this from the fact that in paradise, Adam was not created in his consummated situation. By virtue of creation he lived in paradise with integrity and holiness, in full original righteousness, but still not as though he had already reached the highest condition for which he was destined.

That exalted condition was not yet reality for him, but was held out to him as an ideal. The meaning of the probationary command was precisely that only through his moral victory would Adam have ascended to that highest glory.

Three stages are to be distinguished then: first, the paradise situation; second, the condition of perfect glory; and third, as something in between, the situation in which we now find ourselves, one that did not exist in paradise and is not yet the condition that will come. So in paradise, a higher beauty must have radiated than the beauty now surrounding us. But the beauty that will soon shine forth in the kingdom of glory will far surpass even the beauty of paradise. Between those two there now stands the marred beauty of our sinful condition, a situation that, no matter how lovely and exalted it may still be, nevertheless no longer corresponds to what once existed, and is far from reaching the beauty that will soon be revealed to us.

We can observe still more variegation in that "in between" stage where we now live. This arose directly as a consequence of the fact that the curse did not proceed unrestrained. The unmitigated curse would have changed this entire earth into nothing less than a chaos of ugliness and a desert of corruption. But common grace entered at this point. So the earth did not become those things. The curse is observable everywhere, but was restrained in its operation, and thanks to that preserving operation of common grace this world can still display to us so much beauty. Nevertheless, beauty no longer adorns the whole earth. On the contrary, we discover alongside each other the beautiful, the ordinary, and the ugly.

A lion is beautiful; a calf is ordinary; a rat is ugly. The same holds for the plant kingdom. The cedar enthralls us with beauty, the willow strikes us as ordinary, and the thistle turns us off. The Arab attracts with his beautiful form, we Dutch are rather ordinary in appearance, while some primitive tribesmen arouse a sense of aversion. You find this same threefold categorization not only among plants and animals, but even among nonorganic nature. Some mountain ranges inspire worship. Then there are very ordinary humpbacked mountains that you scarcely notice as you walk past them. There are wild rock crevasses so barren and awful that they arouse an involuntary shudder; these are real specimens of the "formless and void" that once existed. Similarly you find next to the lushness of nature in one region the bare flatness of another region, and next to that terrain you find the barrenness of heath and desert. This is true of the atmosphere as well. Some days you enjoy the kind of sky and weather that make you smile and lift your spirit to the heights, followed by other days that are rather ordinary, when it does not rain and the sun and moon make their appearance. Then you face the days when the stormy winds splash the rain against you and the walkway underfoot becomes impassable.

In those three phases the activity of common grace swings restlessly back and forth in terms of the beauty of nature. Repeatedly God shows you and gives you a sense of what your lot on earth would be, and how ugly the world would be, if the curse had been carried out to its ultimate conclusion. And then God lets you behold an exhilarating natural phenomenon that makes you homesick for paradise. Then you sink again back into the ordinary where nothing excites you or repulses you, but instead where everything around you lacks any vitality and chills your enthusiasm.

The most remarkable feature in this connection is that the sense of beauty has remained the most refined and best developed in regions where nature displays these swings most clearly. In the Eastern world, where civilization is bathed in greater beauty and wealth, the development of the aesthetic or sense of beauty has not disappeared but neither has it been known to rise to heights of creative power. The deficit in this regard is still greater in the upper northern regions where the phenomena of nature are rather unfavorable. By contrast, you find the most glorious human development, also in the area of beauty, precisely in those middle regions between North and South, where the contrasts in nature are constantly displayed side by side, where the three phases we identified are experienced in turn, each in its own way.

From this it becomes evident that common grace has performed a twofold service with respect to beauty. First, common grace has spared much paradise beauty and preserved it from loss, and continues to supply us along our life's way with such a rich treasure of beautiful things in nature. Common grace has tempered the curse and in this way left us with genuine poetry within nature. One and the same stem holds both the unfurled rosebud and the wounding thorn. Second, within the sinful human being common grace has preserved from complete loss the sense of this beauty in nature.

COMMON GRACE HAS SPARED MUCH PARADISE BEAUTY AND PRESERVED IT FROM LOSS, AND CONTINUES TO SUPPLY US ALONG OUR LIFE'S WAY WITH SUCH A RICH TREASURE OF BEAUTIFUL THINGS IN NATURE.

To be sure, our sense of beauty has suffered as well. Numerous people who stroll every evening under God's firmament can do so without ever lifting their eyes to worship God in the splendor of his starry sky. There are even people who have cultivated a desire for the vulgar and disgusting.

But in humanity as a whole, the notion of beauty has been preserved. It is still there. It still operates. That continuation of the sense of beauty is due in no small measure precisely to the alternation of the three phases that we identified. Eyes filled with a view that is brilliantly splendorous will become blind and, conversely, eyes too long in darkness will suffer damage. But when our eyes enjoy alternating views, including ordinary color and plainness, those contrasts provide exercise needed for clarity of vision. We have been given the eyelid for keeping us at night, thereafter to open for us the daylight.

For that reason we do not deny that God has worked inwardly by his Spirit among people in order to fortify this sense of beauty. You see this with Oholiab and Bezalel, and this still appears in the artistic genius of many people.* But without doubt, arranging alongside each other and after each other beautiful, ordinary, and repulsive phenomena has stimulated the sense of beauty. People saw variety. That variety was instructive. Exactly that vision and sense of variety became the powerful incentive to which, as a subsequent chapter will show, art owes its existence and its eminence.

*See Exodus 31:1-11.

eight
GLORY

For he [Abraham] was looking forward to the city that
has foundations, whose designer and builder is God.
Hebrews 11:10

CR

SUMMARIZING what our investigation has taught us thus far, we obtain these conclusions:

1. Despite the fact that it is repeatedly abused by sin and Satan, the realm of beauty, together with the beauty in and of the world, proceeded in its origin and essence from God's decree, and is to be valued as his creature.

2. By the term *beauty* we are to understand what Scripture calls the "divinity" that shines through in the creation in terms of God's eternal power, involving not merely its wise plan but also its outward appearance.

3. In paradise all creatures were beautiful, without blemish or defect, but for that reason nevertheless still not displaying divine beauty in its consummate perfection.

4. After humanity's fall from God in sin, when the curse spread across the earth, beauty diminished and ugliness and hideousness emerged.

5. Had the outworking of this curse continued unrestrained, all beauty would have been replaced by ugliness, even as hell is always accurately portrayed as consummate ugliness.

6. Meanwhile this fatal outworking did not continue unhindered, but was arrested by common grace, and thereby a world exists that displays that triad: the beautiful, the ugly, and the ordinary that neither repels nor attracts.

7. At creation a sense of this divinity that is located in the form and the appearance of things was created within human beings, such that one of the features of our creation according to God's image consisted in the sense of beauty.

8. This sense of beauty was darkened by sin, and would have been lost entirely if common grace had not preserved it for us in part.

9. As a consequence of this, a threefold variety is found among people, namely, a very refined sense of beauty in a few people, indifference toward finer beauty among many people, and pleasure in what is unsightly among depraved people.

10. This state of affairs is not destined to last forever, but will be terminated by a universal cosmic fire, and from this cosmic fire a new world will come forth that will give us to see nothing but perfected beauty, and this perfected beauty is called the "kingdom of glory."

11. In that kingdom of glory, reborn people will exist not only with a sinless soul but also with a glorified body, and with that glorified body will be given the capacity for enjoying and treasuring in a manner that is complete this perfected beauty, namely, glory itself. Thus we will not enjoy a return to the paradise situation, but will enter a situation far surpassing paradise.

Having laid this foundation, we will not pause any longer to consider of what beauty consists. One could write volumes on that issue, and never arrive at a definition. One can say that beauty is born of harmony, symmetry, and proper proportion. But this does not get us very far.

People have indicated what relationships arise in connection with what impresses us as beautiful, but that brings us no closer to a definition of beauty. Even by applying the so-called golden ratio, one can show that the proportions of the golden ratio bring about a beautiful effect, but why this effect is beautiful cannot be rationally explained. We experience this same difficulty with love, something you can enjoy and express but cannot analyze, since it escapes your observation while you are explaining it. Beauty is the way it is because God was pleased to make it so. And we have a sense of beauty because God created that sense of beauty within us.

But beauty does not belong to the phenomena that can direct our thinking in terms of rational concepts. It belongs to the world of imagination, which is distinct from our conceptual world, even as the same is true of the world of love and of every moral quality. So it is a genuine lacuna that within dogmatics and within psychology in general, people have failed to take this world of imagination into account. There is a spiritual-internal world, and there is an external world that appears in visible or audible form, and all beauty consists in the effulgence of the divine in this observable world.

THERE IS A SPIRITUAL-INTERNAL WORLD, AND THERE IS AN EXTERNAL WORLD THAT APPEARS IN VISIBLE OR AUDIBLE FORM, AND ALL BEAUTY CONSISTS IN THE EFFULGENCE OF THE DIVINE IN THIS OBSERVABLE WORLD.

This automatically leads to the question whether beauty consists in this spiritual reality. Linguistic usage actually assumes that it does. People talk of a beautiful character, a beautiful act, a beautiful thought, even a beautiful soul. In that sense it would hardly be impertinent to say that God is beautiful. Nevertheless people tend to be cautious at this point.

Formerly people who were Christians never used such an expression, having been influenced by the school of Platonism that had assigned a spiritual interpretation to the concept of beauty, by speaking about the so-called "beauty-good."* Now this does entail a partial truth, namely, to the extent that beauty finds its origin in God, the basis for that must be spiritual, even as it is not our eye nor our ear but our soul that, by means of ear and eye, observes and enjoys beauty. Still, in that sense people could just as well say that a piece of metal is spiritual, too, since metal has also been created by God, and the spirit within us forges, casts, and forms that metal by means of our hands. This view, therefore, leads to nothing but confusion.

The created world immediately displays to us the contrast between the visible and the invisible, between the material and the spiritual. Unique qualities appear with each of these pairs: matter is heavy or light, hard or flexible, and thus also beautiful or ugly. By contrast, the spiritual is good, wise, ingenious, sinful, or holy. Each of these two elements of creation has a proper series of terms whereby we express its characteristics, and it simply generates confusion if we intermingle these characteristics for both. Our age attaches disproportionate value to art and to beauty, from which emerges the notion that, in the estimation of many, beauty has become the all-surpassing characteristic. The characteristic of "beauty" is applied to the spirit as well, in order to elevate the spirit as being extraordinary. When applied to the highest ideal, as they term it, in their estimation it means little that God is almighty, wise, compassionate, and gracious. Thus they suppose it to be something far superior to say of God that he is comprised of all that is beautiful.

We need to warn against this overemphasis.

---

*Greek: *kalokagathon*

142

Certainly beauty exists in God, and God alone will one day bring beauty to its consummation in glory. But beauty and glory nevertheless remain characteristics of the outward appearance of things, a characteristic that can be applied only figuratively to the spirit. The spirit is not only capable of being wise, ingenious, pure, and holy, and exuding love, but the spirit also comes to expression in relationships, in proportionalities, in specific dimensionality. Because material things display beauty in terms of proper relationships, pure proportionalities, and specific dimensions, people choose to apply the characteristic of beauty to the soul as well, when it displays a proper balance and expresses itself in loving capacities.

THE WORD IS THE MATERIAL WITH WHICH POETRY IS CREATED, YET THE WORD ITSELF IS NOT SPIRITUAL, BUT IT IS THE MATERIAL GARMENT OF THE SPIRITUAL THOUGHT.

Nevertheless, we should attach nothing more than a figurative significance to this. No one has ever thought of treating such dispositions of the soul within the discipline of aesthetics or the study of beauty. When Holy Scripture describes the kingdom of glory for us, comparing it to a city "whose designer and builder is God" (Heb. 11:10), then just as with the description of the New Jerusalem in Revelation 21, we are not to think of the holiness of the blessed, which is expressed with an altogether different image, but rather we are to think exclusively of the new earth under the new heaven, which will have outward and observable form, even as material things are audible and observable for us right now. Only the art of poetry can be identified as purely spiritual, though this too rests on a misunderstanding. The word is the material with which poetry is created, yet the word itself is not spiritual, but it is the material garment of the spiritual thought.

Having now come to speak of art as such, its place is automatically identified. We live in a world that provides us a glimpse of much that is beautiful, but not of beauty in its consummate state. Nevertheless, a homesickness for that consummate beauty dwells within our heart. That heart impulse leads to attempts to conjure up that elevated beauty for eye and ear. From such endeavors art is enlivened.

As will be seen, with these observations we have not said all there is to say, but we can nevertheless deliberately place this eminent starting point in the foreground. The motive of art comes to us not from what exists, but from the notion that there is something higher, something nobler, something richer, and that what exists corresponds only partially to all of this.

THE FEW DIAMONDS AND PRECIOUS STONES THAT WE DISCOVER ON THIS EARTH ARE MERELY THE SCATTERED SIGNPOSTS OF A NEW JERUSALEM CONSTRUCTED SIMPLY WITH PRECIOUS STONES.

The nonbelieving artist may seek that in the ideal of beauty, whereas we who live with Scripture call that higher beauty the beauty of glory that will one day appear. For us, all art and all beauty that proceed from nature constitute a prophecy and foreshadowing of that coming glory. For us Christians, therefore, art exists in direct connection with our expectations about eternity. With trembling hand, as it were, art reaches out toward the glory that through Christ will one day fill heaven and earth.

Scripture tells us that the few diamonds and precious stones that we discover on this earth are merely the scattered signposts of a New Jerusalem constructed simply with precious stones. Similarly, in its most eminent products, art lets us behold only scattered images that help us gauge and grasp something of what will appear in the kingdom of glory.

Let us clarify this with a few examples.

On this earth, beauty is scarcely displayed to the highest degree in the human body and in the human form. But on the new earth, we will be in a position to enjoy a glorified body, one that for the first time will radiate human beauty in perfection. Between both of these we presently enjoy the products of great sculptors and painters, artists who display to us human beauty and the human form with a sublimity and majesty that surpass reality, reaching out toward the glory that one day we will radiate physically. So from a Christian perspective, art not only possesses a sacred origin in the impulse that has been embedded within our heart, but art also enjoys a direct connection with our expectations for eternity. To a certain degree, art forms a bridge between life here and life on the other side of the grave.

Among Christians, every form of denigrating art originated especially in the view that, contrary to Scripture, imagined such life on the other side of the grave to be exclusively spiritual life, a view surrendering any expectation regarding the kingdom of glory. Naturally, if, as spiritualism claims, no observable world will exist in eternity, then indeed art belongs to the lower matters. If, contrary to this, you confess with Scripture and on the basis of Scripture that there will be a new Jerusalem, located on a new earth, under a new heaven, then art is a preliminary scintillation already in this earthly life of what is coming.

If these observations have identified the position of art in our Christian world-and-life view, then at the same time they express why we are in principle opposed to those who assign to art as its highest duty what is called *mimesis*, or the imitation of nature. Among the Greeks already, people considered it the highest achievement if one could paint a cluster of grapes in such a way that birds would be fooled into flying into the painting to pluck those grapes. Nevertheless, one cannot suffice simply with condemning this standpoint. Rather, it deserves appreciation in terms of its significance, which consists in this, that any artistic attempt is futile that conjures up art from one's own ideas separate from beauty in nature. People recall the monstrosities to which this approach has led, especially under the inspiration of the asceticism of the Middle Ages and in the preceding century under the influence of Hegel.* Our purpose will not permit us to discuss this further. Suffice to remark that such attempts did possess this benefit, namely, that such art did strive toward something that went beyond reality, but it failed to satisfy the law of beauty in nature. Following this path, people ended up celebrating the unnatural and the monstrous. In response to this art form, the school of imitational art was entirely legitimate. It summoned art once again back to nature, and compelled art to learn its lessons from nature. We heartily celebrate this development. Only in this way is the artist's talent exposed to the reality of beauty.

Art may not remain at this point, however. The forms of the human body must not be fantasized in a fanciful way, but must be studied anatomically and copied from the living body. But art has a still loftier calling than to put photographs of visible beauty on the canvas. Art fulfills its calling only when it conjures the human form before the eye in terms of dignified harmony and nobility. When it does not serve this function, art denigrates itself even

---

*The German philosopher Georg Wilhelm Friedrich Hegel (1770-1831) sharply criticized the idea of making *mimesis* the sole goal of or evaluative standard for art, arguing that "even if external appearance in its naturalness constitutes one essential characteristic of art, still neither is the given natural world the *rule* nor is the mere imitation of external phenomena, as external, the *aim* of art." See Hegel, *Aesthetics: Lectures on Fine Art*, vol. 1, trans. T. M. Knox (Oxford: Clarendon Press, 1998), 46.

before being aware of doing so, and lapses into portraying nakedness not in its lofty dimension but in its sensual form, succumbing to impurity.

In order to evaluate this issue further, however, the question must be asked: if the paradise situation had been perpetuated, and the contrast between beauty and ugliness had not arisen, would art have been born?

One could ask: if art offers merely a foreshadowing of the coming glory in contrast with the inferior beauty of the sinful world, what calling would art have had if no sin had come, and the beauty of paradise had covered all the earth? In connection with this we recall what was defended in our earlier section, namely, that despite its superior condition, the beauty of paradise was not in any sense yet the kingdom of glory.

Paradise was the starting point, not the destination, of travel. Suppose, then, that no sin had entered the world, and that no curse had made ugliness to appear, even then for humanity there still would have been a difference between beauty at its beginning on earth and beauty in its consummation when glory appeared. This difference would have awakened at a conceptual level a yearning for the ideal beauty of glory. So in this way art would have had its calling to ascend from what existed to the higher level, in the manner of foretaste and prophecy. We are not saying that for this reason art would have functioned in a way similar to its current function. It would probably have enjoyed more eminence, more freedom, more independence, and would have produced results that would have surpassed the loftiest products that we owe to art today. But at no point can it be claimed—and this is our only point in the present context—that in a world without sin and curse, one that had persevered in its paradise situation, there would have been no place for the appearance of any art.

ART IS NOT A NEW INSTITUTION THAT WAS INTENTIONALLY CALLED INTO EXISTENCE BY COMMON GRACE. FAR MORE IS ART A PART OF CREATION ITSELF, JUST LIKE THE LIFE OF THE FAMILY.

We are also not claiming that art owes its origin to common grace. Unlike the state, art is not a new institution that was intentionally called into existence by common grace. Far more is art a part of creation itself, just like the life of the family. Art owes its flourishing to common grace only to the extent that had not sin and the curse been restrained, beauty would have been corrupted, lost to absolute ugliness, and the sense of beauty within us would have been destroyed.

That this did not happen, but that much beauty has survived, that the sense of beauty continued to function, and that art did not disappear but developed, growing and flourishing in strength, for all of this we know ourselves bound to give thanks for God's common grace.

If art is to be traced to creation in this way, then the automatic conclusion is that art must find its origin in our creation according to God's image. Only by acknowledging this can one penetrate the unique secret of art. Art is derived from ability, and such a derivation in its main trajectory is never misleading. The fact that art blossoms among people signifies then nothing else than that the person is able to do something. The word *art* is used in this way even today in various contexts and circumstances. A magician and an acrobat are able to do what you cannot, and each demonstrates his art. In solving a puzzle, the art consists in achieving the purpose of the puzzle.

We have a proverb: "The art is in the getting." Similarly, in every area of activity the expression "that is the art of . . ." is used to indicate that one must be able to do this or that. This general concept, however, must undergo further qualification in order to move from that general ability to the specific ability of the sculptor, the painter, the singer, and so on. People commonly speak, therefore, of fine arts, in order to distinguish art proper from various other skills and tricks. Especially nowadays, now that the application of art to industrial or practical uses is increasing so rapidly, this distinction between art in its refined sense and various practical skills deserves appreciation. There is the art of cooking, the art of horsemanship, the art of fencing, the art of dancing, and many more, but all of this has nothing to do with art. Kant may well have gone too far with his qualification that beauty refers only to what "serves no use," and may have discredited at least architecture.* Nevertheless, the notion of liberal arts contains the basic supposition that art labors for the sake of beauty and not for the sake of the uses in the service of which we might put beauty.

Taken in this way, the ability expressed in art can be understood in no other way than as resembling God's ability, something obviously valid as long as it is understood according to the measure of our human limitation. Since we are created according to God's image, we must be God's followers like beloved children. To be called children of God is our boast, and if Jesus gives each of us the summons, "You therefore must be perfect, as your heavenly Father is perfect" (Matt. 5:48), then it agrees entirely with this calling to understand human art as an adumbration of God's ability.

This needs further qualification, however. God can love; God can reconcile; God can condemn; and yet, even though the

---

*The German philosopher Immanuel Kant (1724-1804), in his *Critique of Judgment*, claims that beauty is "formal subjective purposiveness" (§15), but not perfection. Thus, it is "purposive without purpose" (§10), meaning that for it to be intelligible to us we must assume it to have been purposefully designed (though there is no way of knowing whether or not this is actually the case) while yet having no apparent, definite purpose for which it was designed.

WE CAN FASHION AND PROCESS THINGS THAT EXIST, BUT ONLY GOD CREATES.

capacities for each of these have been placed within us, that is not what we understand by art. No, when we conceive of art as an imitating of God's ability, then here we should think exclusively of that loftiest ability of God that comes to expression in his creative omnipotence. We can fashion and process things that exist, but only God creates. That is his divine ability *par excellence,* the ability of God that distinguishes his work from all human work.

In this sense we now arrive at a further qualification, namely, that taken in a more refined sense, art is the expression of that wonderful capacity within man whereby he can do what otherwise only God can do, that is, create. Language itself teaches us that the notion of creating is always applied among all people groups in terms of art in its more refined sense. The "creations of art" is a shared expression. To say that someone possesses "creative genius" is the highest compliment you can give a real artist. So language itself teaches us that the ability to make art must actually be sought in this creative capacity.

Naturally we do not intend by this to claim that man can create like God creates. Man creates only the semblance or the facade of something. The young bull by Potter is a wonderful creation, but exists only on the canvas.* The animal is viewed in its semblance, but it does not exist in reality; it has no substance. A landscape by van Ruisdael is beautiful; it represents nature before

---

*The Dutch printmaker, painter, and draftsman Paulus Potter (1625-1654) painted *The Young Bull* in 1647. Today, it is classified as an example of early Romanticism. In the nineteenth century, it was as well-known to the Dutch as Rembrant's *Nightwatch.*

your eyes, but it is merely the display of colors and lines, of plants and animals.* No human artist can create substance and splendor in reality; only God can do that. Even though art is actually a life expression that shows that people created in God's image can create like God, nevertheless with people it always remains a creating in a creaturely manner, creating out of imagination, creating for appearance to the eye, creating the representation of the thing rather than the thing itself. God creates the human being, but the sculptor creates an Apollo or Venus, from marble, in lines and forms, but without a human being existing in the sculpture. God creates plants and animals, and the painter knows how to create them in forms, lines, and colors, but without an animal or plant existing in the painting. God creates history, while people create an epic or a drama, drawn either from God's history or from unreality and pure fiction.

WITH PEOPLE IT ALWAYS REMAINS A CREATING IN A CREATURELY MANNER, CREATING OUT OF IMAGINATION, CREATING FOR APPEARANCE TO THE EYE, CREATING THE REPRESENTATION OF THE THING RATHER THAN THE THING ITSELF.

Thus, in all art we find an imitation of the creating ability of God. His universe is replicated in our palaces and cathedrals; his organic creation is imitated in our sculpturing; his landscapes of life in nature and among people are portrayed in our artistic painting on a canvas; what God created and sustains within the human heart sounds forth in our music; and what God created through his word finds expression in our poetry.

---

*Jacob Isaakszoon van Ruisdael (c. 1628-1682) was a Dutch Baroque painter, famous for his landscapes.

But all such creating through art remains limited to the boundary of the human. All of it is creating from God's creation, imitating God's creation in semblance without being able to supply the substance, which proceeds only from God's eternal power. Even as we can certainly make a music box, wind it up, and let it play, we are also impotent when it comes to creating one tiny nightingale or one meadow lark. Similarly, in the entire field of art we can get as far as imitating God's creations without ever getting beyond the imitating. God alone remains the Original, the only Real Creator, for he alone is the powerful and wise Artist.

Now do not complain that we have returned to the imitation theory of art. The imitation theory of art never talks about imitating God, but about imitating nature. This is precisely what makes all the difference. In nature, all of the creating capacity of God has not yet come to expression, for we are still awaiting a higher re-creation. Even as the Preacher of Ecclesiastes has said, God "has put eternity into man's heart" (Eccles. 3:11), so it is that in this area of art, God the Lord has put the sense of beauty in man's heart, a capacity for perceiving a higher beauty than what nature shows us. The perception of this higher beauty is tied, of course, to the real beauty of nature, for art derives its form and themes only from nature.

But fantasy and imagination nevertheless function so powerfully within us that, so long as they are nourished by the beauty of nature, they can ascend to still loftier apprehensions. God himself inspires those who have breathtaking genius in the field of art. He makes them to see a beauty and to experience in their spirit something far beyond what the world can offer, something that, once it moves from their imagination to outward expression, enriches the world, delights those initiated into its meaning, and contributes to our human living something we never would have enjoyed were it not for this artistic capacity.

nine

CREATIVITY

The women at home divide the spoil—though you men lie
among the sheepfolds—the wings of a dove covered
with silver, its pinions with shimmering gold.
Psalm 68:12b-13

CR

NOT SATIATED with the beauty of nature, art reaches for a higher, richer beauty, a beauty that will arrive only with the kingdom of glory, but a beauty that already now supplies prophetic glimmerings. So art is not called merely to produce copies of nature, but to go beyond nature, provided that it ascend to that higher level by means of the ladder of nature, the *scala creationis*. Conversely, nature supplies impressions of beauty that call for art, so that a more ideal position may be attained than what nature offers. The reason that art can serve this purpose is because it owes its appearance to the image of God according to which man has been created. Among the features of this image is the feature that as God creates, so too man creates, by means of creativity in human terms. God creates in reality, people create in semblance. God created the living person in the individual of Adam, the artist creates the human image out of marble.

Indeed, even though this identifies for us a firm and clear position regarding the doctrine of beauty and art in the light of Scripture, nevertheless the significance of art is scarcely illumined with any completeness by this explanation. "For the creation," says the holy apostle, by which he refers to all creatures, "waits with eager longing for the revealing of the sons of God. For the creation," he continues, "was subjected to futility," but it perseveres "in hope that the creation itself will be set free from its bondage to corruption" and thus will share "the freedom of the glory of the children of God" (see Rom. 8:19-21). In the same vein, prophecy proceeded from David's harp to Israel's ear: "The women at home divide the spoil—though you men lie among the sheepfolds—the wings of a dove covered with silver, its pinions with shimmering gold" (Ps. 68:12-13).

Human art, therefore, has the calling to ennoble nature and along with it, human existence on earth. Flowers like those grown in our laboratories are unknown in uncultivated nature. Species of animals are similarly bred through human art for more pure and beautiful species. What goes for plants and animals applies as well to untamed nature, which surely displays a unique beauty while also showing another face than the landscape improved through human art. Anyone who compares the Jotunheim Mountains and the Hardanger region in Norway with the regions of Gooi and Arnhem in the Netherlands will sense the difference immediately. The one displays a more intense majesty, but the region that has lost its ferocity shows more loveliness and tenderness. The majesty of the one makes you shiver, while the beauty of the other attracts you.

This same thing is true of man's own existence. An undomesticated native makes an entirely different impression than a seafarer, and a sophisticated person from an aristocratic family makes an entirely different impression than a person dressed in the splendid finery of local costume.

Repeatedly you see how art functions among both groups, to elevate life to a more noble position in terms of clothes and jewelry, in terms of homes and furnishings, in terms of the manner and style of living. Human life in the African city of Timbuktu is not comparable to life in an Islamic city like Tunis, and the latter fades in comparison to the luxury and beauty that human life displays in cities like London and Paris. In every one of these places, art serves an important function. The art of building, the art of weaving, the art of decorating, to name a few, have been practiced for century after century increasingly to dignify, enrich, and ennoble our outward human life. Gradually all our human life displays a more beautiful countenance, a more harmonious form. Both of these begin to operate reflexively upon people themselves, such that they begin to adopt manners and forms of life whereby their own style and appearance and behavior becomes more refined. Anyone who compares a portrait of Gladstone with that of the Zulu prince Dingane will appreciate the difference.

Amid all these phenomena, a sense of art was at work, a capacity not limited to individuals but operating among the masses. The art of woodcarving in Switzerland and the art of embroidery in Marken had developed and arisen among the people generally. It expressed an impulse for making existence more elegant and making living more beautiful. Even though less refined tastes occasionally crept in, still it cannot be denied that this universal artistic impulse constituted the broad foundation on which the finer arts rest. Every ancient people sang, every people played music, and even though such song and music remained primitive, still it was popular song and melodies that supplied the impulse for more refined lyrical and musical art.

———

But then the distinction appeared between common art shared by all and fine art animated and driven no longer by common understanding but by higher ideals. Remarkably, the more developed this finer art became, the further popular art regressed. Formerly the populace was much more poetic than now, and artistic capacity among ordinary people was much higher in the time of the Reformation. It was as though the artistic sense shifted from the general masses to be concentrated among individual geniuses, leaving the populace destitute. The populace, once so sensitive and melodious and artistically inclined, has become prosaic all the way down to its speech. Life has become too agitated and restless to afford time and tranquility for the outward expression of deeper sensitivities. At that point art retreated from public life, huddled in its own quarters, having won an independent position in life.

That would have been inconceivable if artists with extraordinary talent and genius had not appeared in the realm of beauty. And who other than God created that genius, through the favor of his common grace? Indeed, it could even be asked whether the Greek world was not as oriented to artistic beauty as the Roman world was oriented to the development of authority and jurisprudence.

In the world of beauty a unique divinely established ordinance operated. Initially that ordinance was a secret, and operated only unconsciously in popular art. But in the Greek world that divine ordinance of beauty penetrated the consciousness of several geniuses. At that point these individuals understood, manifested, and realized that ordinance. This explains why this world's classical beauty lay in Greek art. Not because it was Greek art, but because it had pleased God to bring to manifestation for the first time among that wonderful people the fixed and only governing rules and laws, namely, the divine ordinances governing beauty.

The arrogance of what people call taste wants nothing to do with that. The Latin proverb, *De gustibus non est disputandum*, which means, "There is no disputing about tastes," is the arrogant maxim with which the world often evaluates beauty. "I think this," and, "You think that," are the usual claims whereby each person exercises the right to judge.

Now this does contain a relative truth, and that in a twofold perspective. First, in no realm does the subjective right of agreement function as strongly as in the realm of beauty. This is because the significance of impressions that people receive depends to such a large degree on the mirror of our soul that captures those impressions. Second, and this no less, because rational discussion about beauty occurs only very incidentally and the so-called aesthetic evaluation arises from one's own notion of beauty, which is, depending on how finely developed it is, equipped for a more accurate judgment.

Nevertheless, it may not for a moment be conceded that in the world of beauty, the arbitrariness of each person's taste will reign supreme. Anyone who insists that it will cuts beauty off from God. On the contrary, anyone who confesses with us that God is the Inventor and Creator of beauty cannot doubt that beauty is governed by an objective and impartial standard. Such a person cannot deny that a divine ordinance exists to govern the world of beauty. And such a person will always return to the acknowledgement that the classical foundations of beauty were first clearly grasped in ancient Greece.

Naturally this is not to say that therefore all art must be classical Greek art. In particular, ancient Greece never encountered the loftier motive of Christian consciousness. Moreover, classical art does not exist only to be copied continually in a fashion that is both monotone and uniform. Within the world of beauty, indeed, within the entire world, the richest diversity, a virtually infinite multiformity, obtains again and again with its own style and character. But just like the universal form of the flower lies at the foundation of the diversity of all our flowers, so too all artistic variety arises from fixed original forms, and those original forms in all their precision God has disclosed to our human race through ancient Greece.

When a distinct artistic guild developed in human society, within which art obtained its independent existence, a twofold function emerged from that guild. The art that had arisen sought a connection with the artistic sensitivity of the people, seeking to nurture the people and provide them with enjoyment. In addition, however, animated by a still higher impulse, art was driven to seek art on its own, and in this second stage art brought forth its greatest creations in society, creations that in general had no significance to the populace nor exerted any influence upon it, but constituted a distinct manifestation of human experience that was valued and appreciated only by the chosen few within this arena.

That dual use of art was indicated earlier in the comparison between art and religion. In ancient times, religion had its temple, whose threshold was crossed only by priests and singers, before whose altar the people assembled to witness the sacrifices. So too art had its temple, with its high priests, its officiants and singers, who led their own lives within the walls of the sanctuary, inaccessible to the people, but a temple before whose portals the people assembled in order to be raptured, enriched, and blessed by the priests of art.

It was a life within the walls of the sanctuary of art, accessible only for those gifted with a loftier appreciation for art. But this life also provided an influence that proceeded from this temple among large segments of the population. It is the more or less proper relationship between both of these functions of art that shows its nobility. If in the world of artists there is too strong a pursuit of fame, or worse yet, pursuit of mere money, then art runs the risk of debasement, no longer following the law of more refined taste but succumbing to lower taste, to say nothing of the false taste of what people identify as popular. At that point, the order is reversed.

Artistic genius does not determine taste for society, but the taste of society puts its stamp on artistic genius that markets its products for fame or money. That this evil has crept in today cannot be doubted any longer. Art is expensive, artists are seldom frugal, and the straitjacket of order and rules oppresses them. Since the great multitude does not sacrifice its money to enjoy their art, and since artistic taste becomes less and less ideal as it looks more toward the sensual, a kind of self-denigration creeps into art that ultimately brings it into conflict with morality, modesty, and purity. This is true not only about sculpture and painting, but just as frequently about song, drama, and fiction. Consequently a kind of wildness has entered art, which explains the present inability to generate a unique artistic style in modern life.

The modern publicist Claretie has recently observed, after having seen firsthand the art on display at the Paris exhibition of 1900, "Modern art lacks a soul; it lacks masculine power; it lacks the steadiness of lines."* There is a multitude that has broken with everything lofty and that cares no longer for either religion or art. There is another multitude that has completely abandoned religion and now seeks the ideal in art, but does not seek art's ideal in the lofty and dignified, but in the stimulating, the sensual, and the pleasurable, which calls for satisfaction from below.

The priest of art must stand free, lofty, and independent over against all of that. His is not the calling to feed this confused appetite, but to lead it back to the pathway of genuine beauty. But it is exactly this that people living in the temple of art nowadays refuse. People lack character and they surrender. This evil must not be fought by rejecting every enjoyment that art is called to give.

WITHOUT ARTISTIC ENJOYMENT OUR HUMAN LIVING IS IMPOVERISHED.

On the contrary, without artistic enjoyment our human living is impoverished. Far rather is it an evil that must be defeated by purification, a purification that art will achieve in no other way than by elevating the human person beyond the domain of art, in his religious and ethical life.

---

*The French literary figure Jules Arsène Arnaud Claretie (1840-1913) was a prolific journalist, critic, theater director, playwright, and novelist. Claretie is describing the style of art known as *Art Nouveau*, characteristic of the *Exposition Universelle* of 1900, a world's fair held in Paris, France, from April 15 to November 12, 1900.

If we now return to the loftier artistic sphere within the walls of the temple of art, then we will discover here the requirement that the artist seek beauty in nature and in the hidden world. This beauty must find embodiment in his representation, and he must bring beauty to expression by objectifying it with chisel or paintbrush, with harp or cither, in song or chant. When beauty is thus given birth into a new form for the world from his imagination, he must delight in that beauty *because* it is beauty, worshiping God's glory therein and giving thanks to God for having so equipped his fingers.

Artists who honor these requirements are artists by the grace of God, and they alone will never bow before the tyranny of popular sovereignty in the realm of art. Almost without exception the boast can be made of the stars of the first order in every field of art, that in their deepest life principle this is how they became the artistic geniuses of the world. Their artistic products have become the enduring possession of the human race precisely in this way. To the degree that they were enthralled by chisel or paintbrush or pencil, they housed their objects of art in museums so that the aficionado might take delight in them and the devotee of art might receive his initiation in them. As a result, the monetary return grew as nations competing with each other for such select works offered increasingly higher sums.

Nevertheless, a danger no less serious was tied to this life within the walls of the temple of art. One could term it the clericalizing of art. There was an overestimation of one's own domain, a looking down with conceit upon every lower area of life, every kindred area of life, and even every loftier area of life. Piety, goodness, and everything else were nothing. Art was the highest, art was the one and only thing that mattered, and the priests of art were the noblest of all, judging everyone else and being judged by no one. They were a caste with talent, affected by all the dark sides of caste living, permitting themselves everything, denying themselves nothing, showing everyone in every way, including even personal dress and hair styles, that they were a unique kind of being of a higher order, as though they were supermen, living what the French call the "Bohemian life." This was something that went along with the vanity of mutual admiration, pierced by the bitterness of mutual envy. One yearned to see his bust housed in the Royal Museum already during his lifetime. Another craved being decorated with ribbon after ribbon. By means of the mutual support that artists provided each other, their celebrations had to be expanded into national festivals. The more noble characters and the geniuses of finer development still exist, thank God, but they no longer set the tone.

Naturally the evil that challenges us here is less threatening for the singer than the performer, less for the sculptor than the painter, less for the performer than the actor. But still, this danger appears to be far from imaginary even among poets. It affects even the world of our prose literature. Formerly the Christian sensitivity of the artists provided an antidote. Nevertheless, due to the fact that people denied us the possibility of being both artistic and pious, this combination appears increasingly less and less, so that anyone who holds fast to Christ has seemed all too often unable to offer any resistance at all to the faddish evil prevailing in the artistic world, a wicked evil that he at one time conquered by the power of the cross.

───────

Do not let anyone deduce from this, however, that this explains why art and its objects supposedly ceased to function with blessing. The ministry of art always continued in a priestly fashion through its loftier products, even though the priests of art were themselves hardly aware any longer of this priestly ministry.

Within society, those who see and know more serve in every domain those who saw and knew less. The poor man who had no timepiece, who had to be some place on time, would stop you and ask what time it was, and if you owned a timepiece, you would look at it and tell him. There are only a few fortunate ones who may trace from an observatory the celestial messengers, but who share with us what they saw, and they put an image before us so that in this way we could enjoy what their eye saw. Anyone unable to travel to a foreign country can be transported by their imagination to those lands by means of what others who traveled there have seen, and from what they saw they have told us stories.

The same applies in the world of beauty. The artist has a sharper eye. He sees what you do not see. He has a more fertile imagination and captures in the mirror of his imagination things that escape your notice. He sees more; he sees deeper; he sees better; he sees things in relationship to each other. He receives harmonious impressions, and he objectifies those impressions in a way that nature does not provide, but in a way that he must show in order to let you, with your weaker and coarser and less practiced eye, enjoy similar impressions.

The artist sees. What he sees he captures in his soul. From his soul he incarnates that impression in his imagination. From that imagination he brings it to the canvas, in lines, forms, and colors. It is reproduced for you with such humanity and harmony that you perceive and observe on the canvas what you would never have observed in nature itself. That is the fruit of his effort on behalf of the neighbor. That is the priestly service he renders for us who are uninitiated, even though it is nothing more than showing you a scene from nature, a scene from human life, or a powerful event in a way that the expert alone sees it.

Naturally, this priestly service reaches still higher when the artist with imagination initiates you, the one with limited imagination, or at least with limited creative imagination, into what he saw, created, and enjoyed in his artistic vision. At this point what obtains is not simply what could be observed objectively, but we are given to see what was resolved only in the crucible of the imagination, then what was reborn out of sparkling imagination in higher, richer form. Thus, in this higher life form, the sculptor, painter, or singer sees all of this in the field of his imagination, and what he brings forth in marble, on the canvas, or in his song is something loftier, richer, fuller, and nobler. Through his artistic creation he leads you into the world of that ideal, a world you otherwise would never have enjoyed.

The effect of the musician and singer goes still further. Here art brings forth for you a world of vibrations and movements that by means of the ear are brought into contact with the vibrations and movements of your own soul. Here as well art provides nothing more than appearance, but still an apparent emotion that, if it corresponds to the emotion in your own soul, automatically enters the reality of your own life.

The praise of God can make your chest swell, but in such a way that you are incapable of breathing the melody and the lyrics across your lips, something that satisfies the urge of your soul. If the musical artist has known the very same urge, and a singer likewise, but both are capable of bringing this urge to expression in tone and in word, then it is glorious when you discover such a song and such a melody. The same is true when you hear a practiced musician playing the song and a beautiful voice carrying it, until that tone and voice slip into your soul and senses, so that you enjoy a more lofty exaltedness that otherwise you would never have enjoyed.

So it is with the pain that stultifies the soul, with the luxury that ennobles the heart, with the pity that grips you for the sake of another's suffering. The player or singer translates what you yourself can barely stammer, and does so in rich and fulsome chords, and your soul feels liberated. Even the artist with his pencil provides you such an enjoyment. If resentment filled your heart because of the injustice committed against your fellow tribesmen in South Africa, and you could not express that yourself, then it did you good to see your anger at England's tyranny portrayed by means of a striking image. This effect of art occurs independently of the vanity or the self-conceit of the artist. The only relevant question is whether his heart is echoing what your heart wishes to express, and whether he captured that.

———

For that reason, art continues to retain its incorruptible assignment on sacred ground, not simply for the sake of worship in the sense that all art must shed its glow in the sanctuary. We already indicated why this cannot be, and what principle accounts for the fact that to the extent that people worship more and more in spirit and in truth, religious expression becomes free of the visual character of art.

But three arts continue to be summoned into the service of worship. Architecture ensures that harmony exists between what will occur in the sanctuary and the form that the sanctuary displays, or the harmony between inner and outer. But the art of song and music also serve worship, for there is no worship without praise, and praise requires the best song and the purest musical accompaniment. For our God, nothing less than the best may satisfy us, but obviously not as though architecture, music, or song is allowed to dominate the sacred.

In Christ's church, Christ is king and everything must serve him. An organist playing for herself on that account fails to understand her calling, and the singer who does not write his song in the historic line of the worship tradition does not sanctify but sins if the sound of his voice serves to excite him, and if as he leads the singing he does not lose himself in the worship of his Lord and King.

Nothing is more egregious than seeing choristers perform as though they were birds rather than people, performers who feel nothing of the song they are sing-
ing, who are lost simply in the musical sounds. But as long as that performance of art is avoided like a parasitic weed, the art of music and song remain indispensable for our worship. In Geneva, Calvin focused every effort on seeing to it that the singing of the congregation sounded ceremonious, unstrained, animated, and beautiful.

SONG AND MUSIC MUST SPEAK TO THE HUMAN HEART IN THE FULLNESS OF WORSHIP IN A WAY THAT IMPELS YOU TO WORSHIP.

Anyone who is modest will admit freely that everyone sitting in the sanctuary does not at that moment possess the warmth of attitude required for worship. At that point, the art of music and song must be the means for bringing a worshiper's soul out of the ordinary and the mechanical into passion and activity. Song and music must speak to the human heart in the fullness of worship in a way that impels you to worship. That goal is not achieved if the singing lacks holy passion and music lacks loftier animation.

For that reason, entirely separate from the calling that art has for giving voice to Christian ideals outside the sanctuary, this priestly leading of art must be appreciated in connection with worship, as long as it genuinely seeks to be of service. It was therefore a blunder when the unfortunate appetite migrated to us from Scotland, the impulse to identify the ugly within the church as beautiful, and to ban every form of beauty outside the temple. In Geneva Calvin understood the matter entirely differently. He even ventured to introduce multipart singing. By instinct religion is beautiful and seeks the beautiful.

ten

WORSHIP

And King Solomon sent and brought Hiram from Tyre.
He was the son of a widow of the tribe of Naphtali,
and his father was a man of Tyre, a worker in bronze.
And he was full of wisdom, understanding, and
skill for making any work in bronze. He came to
King Solomon and did all his work.
1 Kings 7:13-14

ᘓ

ONLY ONE MATTER still remains to be discussed, namely, the significance of art for the kingdom of heaven. We are not suggesting that from the rich material belonging to the discipline of aesthetics there are no substantial matters remaining to be discussed, matters that in themselves are extremely important. But all of that remaining material cannot even be sketched here. For since we are discussing common grace with regard to art we are able to deal only with those components of the discipline of aesthetics that are related to common grace. This latter definitely includes the significance of art for the kingdom of God.

Common grace forms a contrast with particular grace, from which the kingdom of God arises; but the value of common grace is correctly understood if it is viewed and evaluated from that higher position. The state, family, marriage, child rearing, society, and science were repeatedly illuminated not only in terms of the operation of common grace, but also in terms of the connection between all of these segments of human living and the Christian religion. This concluding chapter will seek to do the same briefly with regard to art.

In the foreground, then, we discover that art can be an instrument and tool of a twofold spirit. The supposition that because art belongs among the ideal expressions of life, therefore it can do no evil, rests on a misunderstanding.

Art can not only cause much injury, but in fact commits much evil. It is a culpable superficiality that so many art lovers among the Lord's redeemed still refuse to acknowledge this. Do not take this wrongly. No serious person will disagree that in its deformation and due to the sin of its practitioners, all too often art defies the moral ideal. One really need not be a Christian in order to acknowledge that sad fact.

In the art criticism published in our liberal daily press, people have repeatedly pointed out how, for example, the stage is continually degraded by the rendering of disgraceful performances and the use on stage of foul language. This is perceived so clearly that serious people among art lovers who live entirely outside of a Christian profession have made repeated attempts to restore dignity to the stage, if possible. The fact that this has not helped is due to finances coupled with the public taste. Stage performances are extremely expensive, and their costs can be covered either by subsidies and donations, or by ample admission receipts. If there were a public numerous enough, with enough means and sufficiently disposed toward the ideal in order to honor a noble performance with faithful attendance, then the business could continue. But such is not the case. The larger segment of the public that seeks entertainment from the stage lacks any lofty sense of art, watches only to enjoy and have fun, and does have fun only when amused by nonsense or only when sensually stimulated by the display of cowardly morals. In order to attract, the piece to be performed is forced to prostitute art.

> GENUINE ART IS WELL EQUIPPED TO PERFORM PIECES THAT ENCHANT AND ENNOBLE, FROM WHICH EVERY FORM OF IMMORALITY REMAINS FAR REMOVED.

In addition, the nature of the matter requires that the stage performers who must hire themselves out to exhibit and display such pieces on stage must abandon most of their shame, so that usually the acting society frequently has low morals. All this flows, however, from the misuse of art, not from its proper use. Genuine art is well equipped to perform pieces that enchant and ennoble, from which every form of immorality remains far removed.

A different evil invades even more deeply, one related more closely to the essence of art itself. Let us focus attention at this point on only two dimensions, the first virtually inseparable from the art of acting, the other constantly appearing among sculptors and painters. In connection with the stage no fine art of performance can be achieved unless the stage performer understands that the art requires him to imagine himself completely immersed in the character and existence of the person whose role he is playing. Now imagine someone who from his twenties to his sixties does nothing else than empathize with various characters, first this one and then that one, so that he is always appearing as another person and never displaying his own person. Suddenly you begin to see how unthinkable it is that such a person should develop his own personality.

If every person seriously agrees that forming one's own personality is one of the best marks of nobility, then the question cannot be avoided whether it is permissible that for our enjoyment an entire group of people is consigned to such an impersonal existence.

No less serious is the second evil that we mentioned, one that for sculptors and painters seems frequently inseparable from their art. Much of their study is devoted to the nude model, which means that they hire young men and young women who stand or sit entirely nude for hours in their studios. It is true that a few artists use their own wife for that purpose, but as a rule they hire these nude models for a fee. Who would deny that in this case, art seeks its triumphs at the cost of modesty and shame?

We could point to more things, but what we have mentioned is adequate to give a sense of how, in more than one area, art views the law of modesty and morality as inapplicable to her. This evil already is of a very serious character, and affects art in principle. Art views itself, for the sake of its artistic ideal, as both permitted and obligated to be emancipated from the moral law. Supposedly the law of modesty and shame was not written to apply to art. So far has this gone that one can find in our large museums, surrounded by spectators, young women who are not ashamed to sit painting the private parts of the male figure openly and in full view. People claim that with a refined artistic appreciation, the sensual consciousness gets suppressed, and therefore one cannot expect or require genuine art to be concerned about shame.

ART CANNOT BE EXCUSED FROM FOLLOWING GOD'S LAW, AND ART DISGRACES ITSELF BY SEEKING THAT FREEDOM.

No one will deny that formally this claim contains some truth. By suppressing the personal, in terms of strictly ordinary beauty, apart from hues and colors, figures and forms can be sculpted and painted in such a way that they exclude any sensual effect. But what person who knows anything about artists' studios will argue that such a noble position is the usual rule, and will not instead complain that the more frequent intention is to capitalize on what can stimulate the senses? From the Christian standpoint, therefore, protesting this pretense of art, as though the law of modesty was not created for art, can hardly be vigorous enough. Art cannot be excused from following God's law, and art disgraces itself by seeking that freedom. Anything that cannot be put into an image

172

or onto a canvas without demanding the sacrifice of modesty or injuring shame must simply be eschewed. Art is not autonomous. Art is one of the more refined human life expressions, and all these life expressions are organically related and stand continuously under God's ordinance.

———

Nevertheless, all of this bears merely an incidental character, insofar as some treasures of art exist in connection with which the issue of character or modesty is not at stake. When we claimed that a twofold spirit can dominate art as art, we had in mind something entirely different. In all of its creations, art is the bearer and instrument of a spirit, of an animus, that directs and drives art in a certain direction. With this we are not denying that to a certain point one can conceive of a neutral zone for art, an area where no particular orientation of spirit comes to expression. But we hasten to add that such a zone evaporates under a more casual analysis, and art can scarcely rise to any higher zone before the expression of this or that orientation of spirit immediately becomes unmistakable.

Even with architecture, everyone senses the entirely different spirit that impacts you when the powerful symbolic dome overpowers you in the Pantheon in Rome, compared to sensing the elevation to a higher, holier sphere upon viewing from the outside or from within a Gothic dome like the one in Cologne. Every lofty architectural style embodies a concept, whether it be the notion of authority and of imperialism, or the idea of freedom, or the concept of the heavenly, even the idea of the practical, and so much more.

But the orientation of spirit comes to far more powerful expression in the art of sculpture and the art of painting, in terms of the subjects chosen and the manner employed to represent them. Compare Rembrandt and Jan Steen, and you will be struck by the contrast between pervasive seriousness emanating from shadowy light, and playful abandon.* You encounter the glorification of man, in his form, in his pride, in his elegance, in his luxury, or you sense the soft and tender effect generated by pity for human misery captured in scenes of love and piety.

What comes to such powerful expression with the visual arts obtains still more serious character with the arts of song and music. Here we no longer encounter the visual effect that seeks to arouse our emotions, but we feel the vibrations of voice and instrument that, by penetrating the ear, take residence in the soul, in the heart, in the emotion, which themselves cause our emotions to pulsate and directly affect our emotional disposition. You cannot measure the beneficial effect of listening to the Dutch national anthem, or the harmful effect of listening to the French national anthem. But one thing is sure: the spirit of every age finds its own musical rendition, so different in the days of the Reformation than the revolutionary melody sung at the close of the eighteenth century. If you compare Bach and Meyerbeer, you sense immediately the totally different spirits coursing through them, a contrast that has shaped even the folk tunes.†

---

*The famous Rembrandt Harmenszoon van Rijn (1606-1669) was a painter and etcher of the Dutch Golden age, specializing in portraiture, landscape, and narrative painting, including many biblical scenes. His later work has a markedly somber character. Jan Havickszoon Steen (c. 1626-1676) was a Dutch Baroque-era painter who, though he varied his style throughout his life, consistently painted lively, even humorous scenes.

†The well-known German composer and musician Johann Sebastian Bach (1685-1750) is noted for his many compositions, both secular and religious, of the mature Baroque style. Giacomo Meyerbeer (1791-1864) was a German-Jewish opera composer credited with originating French Grand Opera.

It is therefore so shockingly superficial when people imagine that as long as music is composed by an eminent master, it is no more than music, and consequently that music has a neutral effect on us. The opposite is true. Every kind of music and every song that has any meaning conveys a spirit to us, travels within us on the sound waves of the musical scale, and influences our emotional mood.

In must be conceded, though, that this effect on our mood is not immediately apparent. By the nature of the case, the sensations occasioned within us by music are merely surface sensations. Many people experience the sensations of intense pain or ecstatic joy, struggles with overwhelming suffering or lofty heroism, at a time when their own hearts are in a very ordinary state, such that the first thing they do after hearing such music is reach for a dish of ice cream or a glass of champagne. To some degree it cannot be any different.

But it is untrue that these surface sensations therefore continue to have no effect on our emotions. Repeated exposure to such surface sensations leads our emotions into a discordant condition, weakens our capacity for genuine sensations, and ultimately damages our emotional life. The outcome persistently shows that many a musical fanatic who surrendered recklessly to music has become a victim of his fanaticism. His central nervous system was affected, and despite all of his indispensable talent, he regresses in honor and risks failures in life. The constant extremes stretch his emotional life too far and too widely, closing off the path to the normal, regular, harmonious development of his personality.

WE MUST THEREFORE PERCEIVE EVER MORE CLEARLY THAT THE RELATIONSHIP BETWEEN OUR PERSONAL SPIRITUAL LIFE AND OUR ARTISTIC LIFE IS A MATTER OF UTMOST IMPORTANCE.

We must therefore perceive ever more clearly that the relationship between our personal spiritual life and our artistic life is a matter of utmost importance. As Paul says, the spirit of the prophet must remain subject to the prophet (1 Cor. 14:32); so too in the realm of music, indeed, in the realm of art in general, the artistic genius must be subject to our personality, or else injury to our personal life cannot be avoided.

One can become inebriated with art, and thus lose control over one's self. People lose their balance and art becomes a toy that they idolize. The claim that artistic love leads many into idolatry cannot be seriously doubted. For many people there is nothing higher than art. Everything must be sacrificed for the sake of their art. Art is their highest goal, the end that justifies all means.

Apart from that disruption of harmony in our inner life, however, a disruption repeatedly occasioned by art, the chief harm that art can cause, and does so repeatedly, is the wrong direction in which it subtly drives our spirit. The worship and idolizing of art is limited to a few fanatics, to a few art zealots. By contrast, the wrong attitude that art can arouse subtly affects the broad masses and causes destruction among the multitudes. This is to be explained by the fact that art is designed to be an instrument for making access for the Spirit of the Lord, for inspiring the holy and high ideal, and thereby for glorifying God the Creator in all art. Despite this intention, art can become alternatively an instrument for crowning the spirit dwelling in the depths as master, and thereby turn its artistic products against the Spirit of God.

Naturally, as in the other areas of life, these two spirits are not arrayed in absolute opposition against each other. This array includes a satanic spirit, a sarcastic spirit, a worldly spirit, an indifferent spirit, a narcissistic spirit, and many more. Similarly, over against all of these we find not just a Holy Spirit, but we see that this ideal spirit appears in various ways, as a spirit of humanity, a spirit of righteousness, a spirit of consecration, and so on. Satan stood in direct opposition to Christ only in the wilderness. But even though we encounter here multiple varieties in weakened form, nevertheless it is indisputable that in all of this, two directions are always running counter to each other, so that ultimately these debilitated and diluted manifestations constantly tug our human emotions in the direction either of the spirit from below or of the spirit from above.

Only when one perceives this clearly will one be in a position to evaluate with any accuracy the relationship between art and particular grace, or if you will, the kingdom of heaven. At first, reaction against pagan art condemned, destroyed, and buried virtually all products of human art outside the domain of Christianity. Thereafter the right of existence was granted to an entirely new development of art, one that gave expression to the spirit of Christianized society.

This was imbalanced, but also understandable, and initially inevitable. In its struggle with the pagan world, the Christian religion time and time again encountered artistic life in the temple and at the forum. Understandably, these initial confrontations could not be reconciled with the Christian faith. Christians embodied a different spirit, one that resisted the spirit from below in the bosom of the people. Consequently, the powerful support lodged in the artistic treasures of antiquity had to be withdrawn from that spirit from below. Conversely, support needed to be provided to the spirit of the Christian religion as the only means for supplying the creation of Christian art. It was simply regrettable that this newborn art was too one-sided and too exclusively ecclesiastical.

It was too one-sided, because it initially assumed a hostile position over against the classical art of antiquity, and too exclusively ecclesiastical, because the resources enabling the flourishing of genuine art were available initially only at the heart of church life. The spirit of the Christian religion was still concentrated in the church and its clergy, and had not yet permeated popular life very deeply at all, so it could hardly generate from that popular culture any new creative art. The new conceptual world that the Christian church contributed to society had at this point adopted sufficiently fixed form only in terms of dogma and liturgy, and was thus unable to yield independent results in the realm of art.

The consequence of this was that the supposition undergirding Christian art virtually echoed the commitment of ecclesiastical art in expressing reaction against pagan life, and did so from an imbalanced spiritualistic stance. Conversely, the exclusive nature of this Christian art gave ecclesiastical worship a gradually increasingly visual character. Even though this ecclesiastical art produced much that was undeniably beautiful, while performing a valuable service of providing the idealized view of life a more sanctified direction, nevertheless it can arguably be criticized for not being able to continue opening the path for further development. After all, art lives from common grace, and without people noticing, this ecclesiastical art was able to bring human art out of the realm of common grace into the private realm of particular grace.

This explains why the Reformation broke with ecclesiastical art and refused, despite deep appreciation for the beauty it had brought to expression, to honor it as the only genuine and complete expression of art according to Christian standards.

Two things contributed to this: first, the more spiritual form of devotion and worship that the Reformation placed in the foreground; and second, the need for a more natural and well-rounded expression in the realm of art.

Worship became more sober, so artistic sculpture and artistic painting could no longer adorn God's house. People no longer gave monetary gifts for decorating temple and church. They attempted to practice a devotion of a more inward nature, emphasizing more the beauty of the soul than the beauty radiating from marble or canvas. In addition, people felt constrained by a view of life that had put the ecclesiastical stamp on the entire realm of art. The notion gained currency that human life in all its manifestations constituted by itself a pursuit of art.

No matter how intensely people advanced the ideal of art,

PEOPLE MISUNDERSTOOD THE NATURE OF ORDINARY HUMAN LIFE. PEOPLE WERE EXHILARATED BY AN IDEAL THAT HOVERED HIGH ABOVE US, ONE THAT HAD FOR THE MOST PART LOST REAL CONTACT WITH NATURE AND WITH LIFE.

people still wanted this pursuit of the ideal to remain connected with both feet in real and practical life. People misunderstood the nature of ordinary human life. People were exhilarated by an ideal that hovered high above us, one that had for the most part lost real contact with nature and with life. So this full-orbed human life broke through the ecclesiastical fences. That human life began, with more intense energy, to become conscious of its independent significance and of its indisputable right to independent manifestation. In this way, outside the church and freed from ecclesiastical domination, fresh artistic expression flourished at that point. Emerging from the classicism of ancient Greece under the leadership of the Renaissance and its return to nature, and owing its direct connection with popular culture to the Reformation, this fresh artistic expression opened up an entirely new period for the blossoming of art.

In this way art entered the open market of life once again, though it thereby placed itself once again before the powerful temptation of the spirit from below that constantly besets us in the midst of our sinful human living with respect to every manifestation of human life. Once again art spread its wings in freedom, but that freedom brought with it the danger of misusing artistic talent. Art returned to the territory of common grace, but precisely for that reason ran the risk once again of being infected anew by the raging sin for whose restraint common grace had been revealed. Art became broader in its perspective and wider in its range of activity, but in its broader development quickly saw the merging of that duality of spirit and direction that necessarily arose from the dual streams within the popular spirit.

People greeted the artistic manifestation of palingenesis that exhibited the power of the Christian spirit beyond the ecclesiastical domain. But alongside this they saw a kind of art emerge that partially circumvented the contrast between the sacred and the profane, but unfortunately gradually led to an artistic development that was inspired by the spirit from below.

This is the natural, which will continue in the context of sin until the end. As long as the mixture of the profane and the sacred persists on this earth, and the kingdom of glory, i.e., the highest ideal, is not yet realized, beauty cannot come to unity and harmonious manifestation. Within the world in which we dwell a multiform spirit exercises dominion, and in that spirit world the spirit of Christ and the spirit from below constitute opposing forces that are irreconcilable.

If art were a systematic embodiment of ideas, a kind of enclosure could be erected around it. But that is not what art is. Art does not arise from concepts and is impotent to interpret ideas. Just as ideas arise independently from our thinking, so too for its part art arises out of the world of our sensual imagination. As this spirit, functioning with the tool of imagination, gains clarity and self-awareness, not only personally but also in the fellowship of communal living, then an inner compulsion drives this spirit to manifest itself in the world of beauty, so that what is experienced inwardly comes to be embodied in something accessible to ear and eye.

———

It is therefore a gap in the life of Christianity if, because it is too far estranged from nature and too little interested in the sensate life of the imagination, it should lack the impulse to manifest itself in the world of beauty, under the inspiration of the spirit of palingenesis, thereby to glorify the name of her God in the realm of art. Our opposition toward much that is honored in the world may well explain this gap. But it must still be recognized as such.

In the arena of song and music, thank God, Christianity has hardly lacked its high priests of art, whose thinking has proceeded from the Holy Spirit and who by the inspiration of the Spirit of the Lord have plucked the harp. In this way they produced sufficient evidence that beyond the ecclesiastical sphere, art that is baptized by Christ's Spirit can blossom in higher, more ideal form. But this does not permit us to make excuses for the gap existing in the area of the visual arts.

These arts, though they are lower, nevertheless are no less called to give honor to God who has called us to a more exalted view of life. Only let people be careful not to allow that ancient error to sneak into the visual arts once again, which claimed that the art of painting serves a higher spirit only if it portrays scenes from the Bible, or architecture serves a higher purpose only if it erects buildings for worship. The spirit of Christ ennobles all of life. Someone who regards nature as Jesus regarded it, who then possesses the artistic talent for transferring the received impression to a canvas and helps us to enjoy that impression, has glorified his God as a Christian.

THE SPIRIT OF CHRIST ENNOBLES ALL OF LIFE.

Similarly, someone who is able to understand human life in the wealth of its manifestations and in the multiplicity of its struggles, as that must be understood with the light of God's Word, and who knows how to transfer the received impression into the world of beauty, has interpreted the Spirit of his Lord dwelling within that life.

Ruskin was writing parody when he called us to imitate God in the six days of creation, but in his singular summons lay this valid idea, namely, that if God glorifies himself by creating through his Holy Spirit light amid darkness, the sea amid dry land, together with the plant and animal kingdoms, then every kind of art impoverishes itself and shortchanges the glorifying of God's name if it separates the life of the sacred from the life of nature.[*]

With this our studies on common grace are concluded. If these studies were able to shed light on many profound issues relating to our Christian life, then for such a result may all honor be ascribed to him alone who granted us the time and strength.

---

[*]John Ruskin (1819-1900) was a leading English Victorian-era art critic.

ABOUT THE COMMON GRACE TRANSLATION PROJECT

There is a trend among evangelicals to engage in social reform without first developing a coherent social philosophy to guide the agenda. To bridge this gap, Acton Institute and Kuyper College are working together with other institutions to translate Abraham Kuyper's seminal three-volume work on common grace (*De gemeene gratie*), which has never before been translated into English. *Common Grace* was chosen because it holds great potential to build intellectual capacity within evangelicalism and because a sound grasp of this doctrine is what is missing in evangelical cultural engagement. *Common Grace* is the capstone of Kuyper's constructive public theology and the best available platform to draw evangelicals back to first principles and to guide the development of a winsome and constructive social witness.

Common grace, as Kuyper conceived it, was a theology of public responsibility and cultural engagement, rooted in Christians' shared humanity with the rest of the world. Kuyper did not intend these volumes to be academic tomes. They were popular works—collections of newspaper editorials written over a six-year period—in which he equipped common people with the teaching they needed to effectively enter public life. Kuyper neither politicized the gospel to accommodate his agenda nor did he encourage his followers to develop a siege mentality in isolation from the rest of the world. As Kuyper writes in his introduction to the volumes, "If the believer's God is at work in this world, then in this world the believer's hand must take hold of the plow, and the name of the Lord must be glorified in that activity as well."

This three-year project involves the complete translation of Abraham Kuyper's three volumes, totaling over 1,700 pages. Volume one is scheduled to appear in fall 2012. This publication of *Wisdom & Wonder: Common Grace in Science & Art* represents the first published selection from this broader project.

ABOUT ABRAHAM KUYPER
(1837-1920)

Abraham Kuyper's life began in the small Dutch village of Maas-sluis on October 29, 1837. During his first pastorate, he developed a deep devotion to Jesus Christ, spurring him to a deep commitment to Reformed theology, which profoundly influenced his later careers. He labored tirelessly, publishing two newspapers, leading a reform movement out of the state church, founding the Free University of Amsterdam, and serving as Prime Minister of the Netherlands. He died on November 8, 1920, after relentlessly endeavoring to integrate his faith and life; truly, his emphasis on worldview formation has had a transforming influence upon evangelicalism, through the diaspora of the Dutch Reformed churches and those they have inspired.

In the mid-nineteenth-century Dutch political arena, the increasing sympathy for the "No God, no master!" dictum of the French Revolution greatly concerned Kuyper. To desire freedom from an oppressive government or a heretical religion was one thing, but to eradicate religion from politics as spheres of mutual influence was, for Kuyper, unthinkable. Because man is sinful, he reasoned, a state that derives its power from men cannot avoid the vices of fallen human impulses. True limited government flourishes best when people recognize their sinful condition and acknowledge God's divine authority. In Kuyper's words, "The sovereignty of the state as the power that protects the individual and that defines the mutual relationships among the visible spheres, rises high above them by its right to command and compel. But within these spheres . . . another authority rules, an authority that descends directly from God apart from the state. This authority the state does not confer but acknowledges."

ABOUT THE CONTRIBUTORS

Vincent E. Bacote (Ph.D., Drew University) is associate professor of theology at Wheaton College in Wheaton, Illinois, where he also directs the Center for Applied Christian Ethics. He is the author of *The Spirit in Public Theology: Appropriating the Legacy of Abraham Kuyper* (Baker Academic) and a contributor to *The Gospel in Black and White* (IVP Academic) and the *Dictionary for the Theological Interpretation of the Bible* (Baker Academic).

Jordan J. Ballor (Dr. theol. des., University of Zurich) is a research fellow at the Acton Institute for the Study of Religion & Liberty and executive editor of the *Journal of Markets & Morality*. He is also the author of *Ecumenical Babel: Confusing Economic Ideology and the Church's Social Witness* (Christian's Library Press).

Stephen J. Grabill (Ph.D., Calvin Theological Seminary) is director of programs and international as well as senior research scholar in theology at the Acton Institute for the Study of Religion & Liberty. He is author of *Rediscovering the Natural Law in Reformed Theological Ethics* (Eerdmans) and general editor of the *NIV Stewardship Study Bible* (Zondervan).

Nelson D. Kloosterman (Th.D., Theological University of the Reformed Churches [Liberated], Kampen, the Netherlands) is ethics consultant and executive director of Worldview Resources International, a service organization whose mission is to produce and provide resources designed to assist in understanding and applying a Christian worldview to responsible living in a global culture. He has served as minister and professor for more than thirty years, and translated dozens of works on Reformed theology and ethics.

Gabe Lyons is the founder of Q—a learning community that mobilizes Christians to advance the common good in society and author of *The Next Christians: The Good News About the End of Christian America* (Doubleday). Additionally, he is the co-author (with David Kinnaman) of *UnChristian: What a New Generation Really Thinks About Christianity and Why It Matters* (Baker), a best-selling book based on original research that revealed the pervasiveness of pop culture's negative perceptions of Christians.

Jon Tyson is a church planter and lead pastor of Trinity Grace Church, located in New York City. He is also on the board of directors of the **ORIGINS MOVEMENT**, a new church planting movement committed to multiplying missional church communities in the major urban centers of the world. With Darren Whitehead he is co-author of *Rumors of God: Experience the Kind of Faith You've Only Heard About* (Thomas Nelson).

TOPIC INDEX

SCRIPTURE INDEX

Note: e=epigraph; n=footnote